BUCKNELL REVIEW

New Interpretations
of
American Literature

STATEMENT OF POLICY

BUCKNELL REVIEW is a scholarly interdisciplinary journal. Each issue is devoted to a major theme or movement in the humanities or sciences, or to two or three closely related topics. The editors invite heterodox, orthodox, and speculative ideas and welcome manuscripts from any enterprising scholar in the humanities and sciences.

This journal is a member of the Conference of Editors of Learned Journals

BUCKNELL REVIEW
A Scholarly Journal of Letters, Arts, and Sciences

Contributors should send manuscripts with a self-addressed stamped envelope to the Editors, Bucknell University, Lewisburg, Pennsylvania, 17837.

BUCKNELL REVIEW

NEW INTERPRETATIONS
OF
AMERICAN LITERATURE

Edited by
RICHARD FLEMING and MICHAEL PAYNE

LEWISBURG
BUCKNELL UNIVERSITY PRESS
LONDON AND TORONTO: ASSOCIATED UNIVERSITY PRESSES

Associated University Presses
440 Forsgate Drive
Cranbury, NJ 08512

Associated University Presses
25 Sicilian Avenue
London WC1A 2QH, England

Associated University Presses
P.O. Box 488, Port Credit
Mississauga, Ontario
Canada L5G 4M2

The paper used in this publication meets the requirements
of the American National Standard for Permanence of Paper
for Printed Library Materials Z39.48-1984.

Library of Congress Cataloging-in-Publication Data

New interpretations of American literature.

  (Bucknell review; v. 31, no. 2)
  1. American literature—History and criticism.
I. Fleming, Richard. II. Payne, Michael.   III. Title.
IV. Series.
AP2.B887   vol. 31, no. 2   051 s   [810'.9]   86-48008
[PS92]
ISBN 0-8387-5127-X (alk. paper)

(Volume XXXI, Number 2)

PRINTED IN THE UNITED STATES OF AMERICA

Contents

Recent Issues of BUCKNELL REVIEW

Notes on Contributors

MICHAEL VANNOY ADAMS is an associate provost at the New School for Social Research. His article, "Deconstructive Philosophy and Imaginal Psychology: Comparative Perspectives on Jacques Derrida and James Hillman," appeared in the *Journal of Literary Criticism.*

NANCY PROTHRO ARBUTHNOT has published articles on Wallace Stevens in *The New England Review* and *Concerning Poetry.* She is an associate professor of English at the United States Naval Academy. Currently she is working on a study of the influence of Stevens on David Hockney and other contemporary artists.

RICHARD H. DILLMAN, associate professor of English at St. Cloud State University, is the editor of *The Minnesota English Journal.* He has published articles on Thoreau and American literature in *ESQ: Journal of the American Renaissance, The Thoreau Journal Quarterly,* and *The Midwest Quarterly.*

RONALD EMERICK is the assistant chairperson of the department of English at Indiana University of Pennsylvania, where he teaches courses in American literature and technical writing. He has published articles on Mark Twain, Henry James, and Flannery O'Connor.

BARBARA M. FISHER is an assistant professor of English at the City College of the City University of New York. She is a specialist on Wallace Stevens and Bernard Shaw and has published several articles in *The Wallace Stevens Journal.*

TERRANCE KING teaches at Wayne State University in Detroit. His article, "'Certain Phenomena of Sound': An Illustration of Wallace Stevens' Poetry of Words," appeared in *Texas Studies in Literature and Language.* His work has also been published in *Semiotica* and *The Wallace Stevens Journal.*

LAURA LAFFRADO has written on Nathaniel Hawthorne, the Brontës, and John Winthrop. She teaches at the State University of New York at Buffalo.

ROSANNE WASSERMAN's poems, translations, and articles appear in anthologies and magazines internationally. She teaches at the New York City campus of Pace University and for New York State Poets in the Schools.

O. ALAN WELTZIEN, associate professor of English at Ferrum College, completed work on his article while a James Still Fellow at the University of Kentucky. He has published a number of essays on Thomas Wolfe and Nathanael West and has been a regular book reviewer for the *Roanoke Times and World News* for several years.

Introduction

The essays in this volume offer new interpretations of works by Hawthorne, Thoreau, Melville, Stevens, and Moore. O. Alan Weltzien discovers moments of interrupted festivity as constituting a prominent emblem in Hawthorne's iconographic style. Laura Laffrado recovers the importance of Mrs. Wakefield and the significance of matrimony in Hawthorne's short story "Wakefield." In the similarities between Pearl and Chillingworth in *The Scarlet Letter,* Ronald Emerick finds a powerful instance of Hawthorne's recurring fascination with heredity as a determinant of character. Richard Dillman, in his three-part study of Thoreau's philosophy of rhetoric and style, draws on the complete range of Thoreau's work to reconstruct his views on the art of writing. Drawing on Jung's account of the shadow archetype, Michael Adams proposes an explanation for Ahab's fascination with evil in *Moby-Dick.* Barbara Fisher, on the other hand, casts a suspecting glance at Jungian interpretations of Stevens's interior paramour, finding the poet's main sources in the Bernardine soul as *sponsa,* as derived from the Song of Songs, and in Plato's Diotima. Nancy Prothro Arbuthnot traces Stevens's autobiographical turn in *The Auroras of Autumn,* which he looked on as possibly his last poems. In reaction against Helen Vendler, J. Hillis Miller, and Frank Doggett, who have stressed Stevens's indeterminacy, Terrance King argues that the poet's enigmas can be solved in a way that reveals his deliberate strategy of secrecy. Finally, in her reading of Marianne Moore's "Marriage," Rosanne Wasserman discovers that the poem's meaning arises from a difficult marriage of lexis and structure, which emerges from the complexity of detail in the poem.

At a time when so much attention in literary study has been given to breaks, slippages, and irreconcilable oppositions in texts, these essays emphasize the importance of what can be determined through careful, contextually informed reading. Rather than adopting a reactionary stance against theory, these essays demonstrate the importance of descriptive interpretation for the understanding of literature. Such description, when freed of the blinders that kept the New Criticism from seeing either the author or the audience of a work, remains central to criticism that is conceived as a body of knowledge about literature. Perhaps nowhere else than in literary study is it possible to assess so readily the observational and descriptive adequacy of interpretative statements that propose to advance what is known about a subject by examining the primary documents on which those statements are based. However complex the art of reading surely is and however changeable the meanings of words and the methods of criticism brought to them, the author's text remains a liberating reference point. Rather than binding the students of literature, the text in its accessibility frees them from critical doctrine and priestly authoritarianism. In this way the literary text forms the center of a community of critical readers, who may only rarely meet face-to-face but whose views about their common literary concerns can be shared, understood, modified, and developed.

In the conclusion to his recent study of theory and the study of American literature, *The Unusable Past,* Russell Reising writes, "What is needed is a situating of authors, texts, and genres (of discourses, as Todorov and Hirsch would have it) in a milieu capable of accommodating diverse, often radically disjointed, linguistic works and of generating new appreciations of what might emerge as 'American' about American writings" (p. 229). Such an opening up of the canon of American literature to works and authors who have been previously dismissed as minor is intended to have the effect of "understanding literature as a reflection of American society" (p. 218). There is, however, no need to exchange one strategy of exclusion for another, to recover what has been mistakenly judged unusable by displacing what has been thought central to the American literary tradition. Careful study of the genesis, form, and reception of works that have been valued in the past and of those judged "diverse, often radically disjointed"—without assuming first that those which more fully reflect American society or those which strive to transcend it are of greater value—now seems to be the approach most likely to produce a comprehensive understanding of American writing. In the current critical climate what Marianne Moore said of poems has taken on immediate significance: "these things are important not because a / high-sounding interpretation can be put upon them but because they are / useful."

Michael Payne

BUCKNELL REVIEW

New Interpretations
of
American Literature

The Broken Circle of Mirth: Emblems of Interrupted Festivity in Hawthorne's Romances

O. Alan Weltzien

Ferrum College

I

FROM his arched window in *The House of the Seven Gables*, Clifford Pyncheon watches an Italian organ-grinder's show and cries at its sudden cessation.[1] He has taken pleasure in the miniature community of animated toy figures existing within a mahogany case, and feels revolted by the ugly monkey, the pantomimic epilogue that signifies the purpose of the show, the giving of "filthy lucre."[2] The show illustrates its clichéd moral, the metaphorical dance of life, which Hawthorne's narrator discusses.

For the character the show turns ugly and disillusioning; for the reader it momentarily reanimates a well-worn view of human life. When the organ music stops the "harmonious existence" of the frantically gesturing figures, their "most extravagant life," instantly freezes "into a dead torpor," and we're left facing the monkey and contemplating the vanity of human aspiration. We are also left with the still frame of the frozen moment: from the passing action emerges a permanent emblem.

Hawthorne modeled this brief scene upon an encounter involving himself, daughter Una, and an organ-grinder. A comparison between his 1845 Notebook entry (8:271) and his fictional elaboration reveals him changing the anonymous organ-grinder to a young Italian and, more importantly, adding the show. He creates the miniature community because of his interest in emblems of interrupted festivity. That mahogany case frames a verbally wrought symbolic picture of a type Hawthorne repeatedly devises. I call these scenes emblems because they pictorially present certain meanings it is assumed the reader will recognize and accept.

Emblems invite interpretation of their generally symbolic content; they pack meaning, and Hawthorne's emblems are no exception. Specifically, the emblems of interrupted festivity hold in tension the contrary states of community and individuality, interdependence and isolation.[3] Occasions of festivity or revelry in Hawthorne generally endorse interdependent life even as they display characters losing that life. Forms of play, the joined hands of the circle of dance, even the integrated columns and rows of processions: all signify a positive communal life, an ensemble that clashes with Hawthorne's customary definition of individuality (e.g., 4:113), which isolates rather than integrates the individual.

These emblems, a form of tableaux, ask the reader to apprehend the value of community in the context of individual isolation, which context usually forms the visual center of interest. The moments of interruption record the clash between these contrary states, and the stilled instant of suddenly interrupted pleasure constitutes the essential emblem. Interruption focuses and captures the meanings of both the circle intact and the circle fractured and dissolved. The circle describes ideal life and the broken circle, ordinary life. These emblems absorb the meaning of the action bordering the frozen moment. They concentrate meaning and therefore linger in the mind as visual epitomes of the narrative from which they emerge.

Interrupted festivity, then, distills the Hawthornian contraries of living in step or out of step. Arne Axelsson believes that "the firmer the idea of a work is linked to the conception of character, the more likely it is that the idea is also connected with human isolation and interdependence."[4] Since Hawthorne typically clothes the idea of a work in character, these polarities form a primary—if not the primary—thematic network, and interrupted festivity becomes a distinctive expression of it because of its emblematic concentration.

Among other things, Clifford Pyncheon in "The Arched Window" signifies Hawthorne's reader, who frequently encounters clearly framed pictures of the common motion of common life. We have noted that he cries, as did Una Hawthorne that day in 1845, but the character cries because he has vicariously participated in the "harmonious existence" within the mahogany case, and his imagination does not outlast the music. These figures are but toys, artificial and mechanical, yet as Hawthorne details them, their motions disclose for Clifford and the reader a view of interdependent life. The suddenly halted organ reminds Clifford that he exists ineluctably outside the case and the street, imprisoned in the house.

The company of toys, a production of Fancy's Show-Box, is an emblem of community we apprehend along with Clifford. When the Italian "interrupts" their dance through life its meaning shifts along with our perspective, as we now hover in the street midway between the Italian and Clifford, taking in both the stilled figures and Clifford's tears in one gaze. The arched window frames a picture of individuality just as the mahogany case frames a picture of community. These poised ideas are as important as, if less obvious than, the authorial commentary on the dance of life. That commentary does not emphasize the emblem's reference to character. The figures Hawthorne added, like the political procession and Sabbath bells in the same chapter, confirm the unavailability of life in the street for Clifford.[5]

Most would agree that music is capable of drawing people together physically and spiritually, and the same holds for holiday observances. Both contain a strong, converging energy, a gravitational attraction. This truth exerted some fascination over Hawthorne, who developed it in his fiction with an unusual twist. Pageantry or revelry exists to be interrupted, terminated before its completion. It enjoys a twilight existence. Without some unforeseen intrusion or cessation, festivity might not exist at all; the interruption sanctions the festivity, and in effect one's typical life apart temporarily affords access to an ideal life, the circle of mirth.

Joined hands, or ensemble life, sets off with maximum contrast solo life, our usual lot, and interrupted festivity forms the strongest possible vehicle for defining a character caught between both modes even as he resumes the latter. Stylized movement to music clearly evokes hands joined together. Dance is one of Hawthorne's favorite metaphors for community, though by no means his sole one. Hawthorne favors dance because it is premised upon joy and play, and evokes a golden age, an ideal harmony in space and time or an impromptu eruption of antic motion for its own sake. The measures of the dance gather up individual lives into a common one, and when the measures stop—or when a procession halts—the common life is held in suspension with the individual lives that swiftly replace it.

This attitude toward dance might well have prompted Hawthorne to write "The Masqueraders" (chapter 24) in *The Blithedale Romance* as he did. As with the case of toy figures in *Seven Gables,* the difference between the Notebook source and the fiction demonstrates Hawthorne creating, this time on a larger scale, an emblem of interrupted festivity. As is well known, he modeled the scene upon his own experiences at Brook Farm. From his note about the fantastic "picnic party" he witnessed in the woods there (8:202–3), he borrows some American history and a little literary history and mythology to compose his circle of masqueraders, adding in many figures to those he had seen and thereby creating a larger and more variegated masquerade. Similarly, from the bare suggestion of "childish games, in which grown people took part with mirth, enough," he creates the actual dance (3:194).

The dance exists for its own sake and bears specific meanings for Zenobia and Coverdale, as will be seen. Hawthorne assumes the reader discerns the contrary significances of his emblem. Like all this group of emblems, it proposes conflicting, if not mutually excluding, values. For example, the prose clearly states that their discrete identities, already at one remove *in costume,* wholly disappear in the happy dance, yet the dance retains more than a trace of demonism. Their pleasure is both wholesome and tainted, and such ambivalence characterizes these emblems.

At Brook Farm, strolling in the woods in company with George Bradford, Hawthorne had been playfully engaged by "two denisons of the wild wood," who drew them on "in a lonesome glade" to "a company of fantastic figures." While they romped, Hawthorne, "whose nature it is to be a mere spectator both of sport and serious business, lay under the trees and looked on." Miles Coverdale is not thus engaged and invited forward, and the difference between the author at Brook Farm and Coverdale in chapter 24 exposes and condemns Coverdale's voyeurism. There is no excuse for wallflowers who do not move in step when opportunity avails. Hawthorne watched masqueraders; Coverdale spies on a dance and ends up "a mad poet hunted by chimeras."

But we look with Coverdale more than at him, and we interpret the scene before us from the recess of shrubbery and, retrospectively, from Eliot's Pulpit. Hawthorne makes us, like himself at Brook Farm, the "spectator both of sport and serious business," sifting these opposed meanings contained in all his moments of interrupted festivity. Sport and serious business conditionally define each other in Hawthorne's festivities, most acutely in these frozen moments. Understanding both terms enables us to recognize their connection and thus more fully interpret this group of emblems.

II

Excepting *The House of the Seven Gables,* festivity of some sort climaxes and integrates our cumulative understanding of character in the major romances. Specifically, Hawthorne features contingent and terminated festivity, the occasion for sport, to complete the arcs representative of his major characters. Those arcs usually intersect only in passing. It is as though the serious business that is life infrequently allows sport, which quickly loses ground again to serious business.

Terminated festivity affirms its contingency; interruption forms Hawthorne's preferred language for expressing the temporary license granted sport. Sport wants company; to act in a sporting manner is to take part or take a part. In many respects *The Marble Faun's* Corso Carnival represents the most fully drawn, and most clearly affirmed, festivity in the romances, and Hawthorne's own experiences at the Carnival shed light on the meaning of festivity for character. It is well known that Hawthorne's disapproving heart thawed at his second Carnival (February 1859), which he judged kindly. His change in sentiment, occurring late in his life, provides an insight into his recurring use of transient festivity as one context for defining character.

As the etymology of the word demonstrates, carnivals were originally contingent upon a season of deprivation and sorrow (e.g., Lent) that followed them. Hawthorne accepts that contingency, as he concludes his account of the 1859 Corso by saying, "to-day, we have waked up in the sad and sober season of Lent" (14:505). Before his epilogue, Hawthorne wrote down historian John Lothrop Motley's account "that it was formerly the custom to have a mock funeral of Harlequin, who was supposed to die at the close of the Carnival, during which he had reigned supreme; and all the people, or as many as chose, bore torches at his burial" (14:504–5).

Harlequin, of course, defines the type of the clown, whose pantomiming art rests, in good part, upon adult imitations of children. To clown is to act conspicuously younger than one is, even to evince infantile manners. The contingency of the "sacred hour" of holidays sanctions the deliberate buffoonery of participants (their high spirits). Festivity of any sort is playful to some degree. Even the stately, ceremonial stride of the Election Day procession in *The Scarlet Letter* illustrates figures at play with their individual customary habits. One assumes a role and becomes someone or something other knowing that this "other" enjoys only a temporary existence. It is bound and limited by time.

The Election Day procession frames a worship service and precedes the most serious of political events; the Carnival, depicted in the *saltarello* of Berlioz's Roman Carnival Overture, heralds Lent. The contingency of festivity is spatial as well as temporal, and the mahogany case of toy figures proves the extreme example. The Blithedale masqueraders, already living at one remove from ordinary reality, remove themselves further for their dance in the forest glade. And in *The Marble Faun* Hawthorne reproduces his Notebook observation of the narrow confines of Carnival merriment, which "does not extend an inch beyond the line of the Corso; there it flows along in a narrow stream, while in the nearest street, we see nothing but the ordinary Roman gravity" (14:76).

Play, as John Huizinga observed, is spatially separate from ordinary life.[6] Play is marked off in time and space, and festivity, which encourages modes of ritual and spontaneous play, forms its chief occasion for expression. Unconfined play is not possible for human beings as it is unreal, outgrown in the dawn of life. The contingency of sport upon serious business, or play upon work, which interrupted festivity focuses, rests upon a vision of opposed states of childhood and adulthood. The advent of self-consciousness, in Hawthorne's view, closes off most prospects of ensemble life; thereafter, life is generally lived solo, and at the most the individual temporarily glances backward in time and joins hands.

So the reign of Play unfurls the lingering traces of the child in every adult. But as a rule adulthood precludes rather than complements childhood, so that play, the child's natural mode of conduct, flourishes only temporarily. Adults at play are adults denying their real selves, since mortal life resembles labor rather than frolic, and since, as Hawthorne wrote in "The Haunted Mind," "In the depths of every heart there is a tomb and a dungeon, though the lights, the music, and revelry above may cause us to forget their existence, and the buried ones, or prisoners, whom they hide" (9:306).

Here again Hawthorne's company of toy figures in *Seven Gables* is instructive. They are unreal and parodic, smaller and faster than human beings. Yet their capers individually and collectively express delight; as toys they celebrate the fantasy of an ideal life, where labor turns into frolic. But playing at life is at odds with living it, hence the contingency and cessation of festivity.

The child-man Clifford Pyncheon, the organ-grinder's audience, exemplifies this view of the circle of mirth existing in an Edenic world of childhood innocence. Foreshadowing the dance of the toys, that emblem of community at play, is a scissors-grinder who produces "an ugly, little, venomous serpent of a noise" rather than music. Clifford takes pleasure in the sight that the allegorical sound destroys; he watches "the circle of curious children, watching the revolutions of the wheel" (2:162). He temporarily enjoys it because it lets him glance far back into his unfettered childhood. The adult gazes upon the inner and outer circles, the motion of the inner reflecting the harmony among the outer, himself a centrifugal point outside, looking across his past as he looks down from his arched window.

Hawthorne uses the temporal and spatial contingency of play as a significant frame of reference for his major characters. His children of Harlequin take a brief holiday from responsibility and disport themselves (e.g., Hester's adolescent defiance in and after the forest), but holidays—and holiday spirits—exist apart from real life. In his Corso experiences he was repeatedly struck by its primary appeal to youth (14:71, 83, 497, 504), and he came to admire and modestly imitate that youthfulness. In his fiction, to act young at heart, to assume an anti-adult posture, becomes a defiant but futile act whose futility enhances its defiance. Emblems of interrupted festivity, pitting the "sport of mankind" against its "earnest," record the final graduation of characters into adulthood.

Festivity, then, possesses two significances that collide with each other, and the interrupting moment brings them together. As the home occasion for ceremonial play and a celebration of an ideal, common life, festivity possesses an inherent validity. But it is also inherently transient, fleeting, as it exists outside the traffic of ordinary life. The creative tension between these contrary significances not only provides one avenue for interpreting character, but also illustrates the playful implications of Hawthorne's style, as Albert Blissert states:

> A sportive experimentation with roles and actions . . . also allows the characters to create an alternative reality to those conditions in their lives, which they are no longer willing to accept, and a playful attitude frees them to enact their longings, even when they recognize beforehand the impossibility of success. The play in Hawthorne's writing . . . [also] defines the very nature of his fictive world as a kind of psychic drama, in which the imagination acts out its exaggerated fears and desires, in order to discover the point at which play can merge with reality.[7]

The "alternative reality" of festive occasions consists of a communal life most genially and easily expressed in some sort of play. However, in the spotlighted psychic contest between interdependence and independence, play does not "merge with reality" with happy consequences. The prenuptial reunion of Kenyon and Hilda at the Carnival's climax in *The Marble Faun* is unusual in its smiling benediction. As a rule reality interrupts and replaces play rather than accommodates it. Hawthorne's emblems, as I have said, contain these conflicting meanings of the validity and the transience of festivity.

Hawthorne proclaims the validity of festivity in several ways. Again, his own change of heart toward the Corso affords a biographical explanation of the value of joined hands in this group of emblems. This experience, occurring in Hawthorne's mid-fifties, illuminates these emblems' external and internal affirmations of community. In some cases Hawthorne's narrator explains this value, like a script accompanying the emblem; in others, the emblems themselves project it.

The Carnival convert ended his account by noting: "It is worthy of remark, that all the jollity of the Carnival is a genuine ebullition of spirit, without the aid of wine or strong drink" (14:505). He felt dazzled by the splendors of color and decoration he saw—"Certainly, there cannot well be a more picturesque spectacle in human life" (p. 499)—which seemed to endorse its wholesome purpose. *The Marble Faun*'s narrator similarly endorses the ensemble of merriment, "a sympathy of nonsense; a true and genial brotherhood and sisterhood, based on the honest purpose—and a wise one, too—of being foolish, all together" (4:439).

Foolishness is wise because it is communal and as such offers temporary relief from the usually solitary, usually serious business of life:

> There is a wisdom that looks grave, and sneers at merriment; and again a deeper Wisdom, that stoops to be gay as often as occasion serves, and oftenest avails itself of shallow and trifling grounds of mirth; because, if we wait for more substantial ones, we seldom can be gay at all. [4:437]

Surely this judgment explains in part the energy behind *The Scarlet Letter*'s essayistic interlude on "the forgotten art of gayety" that unambiguously decries the New World's loss of holiday traditions (1:230–32). Gayety, like sport, requires some social context to thrive; pageantry draws people out of themselves.

Parades such as the political procession in Pyncheon Street signify a more obvious solidarity, if a less apparent gayety. Viewed from a proper remoteness, that procession melts "into one broad mass of existence—one great life—one collected body of mankind, with a vast, homogeneous spirit animating it" (2:165). The narrator's instructions for proper viewing slow its motion into an emblem expressing community. With similar effect, the Election Day procession of soldiers of "ancient and honorable fame" and Puritan civic leaders in *The Scarlet Letter* is pictorial rather than dramatic.[8]

"Viewed from a proper remoteness" means, among other things, reading the validity of festivity in the emblems oneself, unprompted by an explicating narrator. I earlier suggested that the whirl of the masqueraders in *The Blithedale Romance* celebrates their group pleasure as it obscures their individual selves. The wild dance represents an hour of genuine happiness for the community. They tolerate, after all, the presence of an unmasked, disillusioning spectator—the eye of common sense encountering nonsense. Hawthorne places Silas Foster by the circle to suggest their present, extreme remove from ordinary reality and their knowledge of that.

When these masqueraders themselves stop their dance and joyfully recognize their own silliness (3:194), we apprehend an emblem of interrupted festivity wholly expressing the positive, communal meaning of festivity. Its usual reference for the individual is absent. The emblem depicts interdependence without independence, play uninterrupted by reality. Too, we infer from a subsequent remark of Hollingsworth's that the dancers are able to resume their pleasure even after Zenobia has had to quit their circle (3:198). Their greater flexibility— their ability to overcome interruptions—bespeaks their greater self-consciousness of themselves masquerading, and Hawthorne does not condemn their innocent good humor.[9]

The impromptu dancing in the Villa Borghese grounds in *The Marble Faun* also celebrates the validity, however fleeting, of "one great life." Hawthorne creates the spectacle of the "festal people" piecemeal so that in its slow survey the eye catches each grouping in a certain attitude (4:87–88). He emphasizes their common identity by having the dancers appear and later disperse almost instantaneously, as does the "vagrant band." Miriam could be speaking for them as well as the Carnival merrymakers when, interrupted by Kenyon in the Corso, she reproaches him, with Hawthorne's full support: "There may be a sacred hour, even in Carnival-time" (4:448). To understand correctly one must take part, not merely from the comfortable recess of balconies but in the jostle of the street, on foot as well as in carriage.

When Hawthorne went about describing that 1859 Corso in his Notebook, he emphasized the challenge of recounting the scene accurately and fully. "The spectacle is strangely like a dream," he wrote: "It is strange how the whole humor of the thing, and the separate humor of each individual character, vanishes, the moment I try to grasp one and describe it; and yet there really was fun in the spectacle as it flitted by" (14:500–

501). Hawthorne's effort to seize hold of its essence parallels his characters' struggles to lose themselves in "the whole humor" of festivity. However valid festivity may be, the play it sanctions is elusive.

So the "individual" meaning contained in these emblems centers on the transience of festivity, and as I have said, interruption confirms its transience. In the frozen moment we see a character's "separate humor" in relief against the "the whole humor" of the ensemble as he is forced to leave off play and accept his particular form of authorial judgment.

In another respect, the moment of interrupted festivity constitutes Hawthorne's pictorial achievement, his successfully capturing both the meanings of community and individuality before the former "vanishes" from the narrative. The moment of interruption represents an intersection of stillness and motion, however stylized, and these poised meanings take on an emblematic permanence similar in its effect and form to the "brede / Of marble men and maidens overwrought" in Keats's "Ode on a Grecian Urn." Hawthorne's emblem emerges just when the circle of mirth loses its center or shape. These emblems commemorate contrary states of ensemble and solo existence in the same way that the urn and Keats's "Ode" arrest forever the otherwise vanishing lives of the individual figures and "little town."

Clifford Pyncheon, we have observed, stands forever outside the circles and processions that draw him but "flit by." The high-spirited Blithedale festivity is interrupted presumably three times, first by the masqueraders themselves and second by Coverdale, a point outside their circle whose answering laughter flushes his cover. We reconstruct the third and most important interruption, Hollingsworth's accusation against Queen Zenobia, after the fact at Eliot's Pulpit, along with Coverdale. From this interruption emerges the emblem. That Hawthorne leaves the reader to imagine the first moments of their encounter makes it all the more vivid. The accuser in effect disrupts the circle by upsetting its center.

In *The Marble Faun* festivity proves more insistently transient. The broken circle forms the visual essence of the Villa Borghese chapters. Like Hollingsworth, the Model—Miriam's persistent shadow—isolates the pair in a "moral estrangement" from the suddenly vanished dancers, and the circle gives way to a line of agonizing isolation (4:98).

Similarly, the Corso chapters coalesce in a final frozen moment as one couple reunites simultaneously with the other's arrest (4:451). Hawthorne thus counterpoints the comic and tragic destinies of the two couples who participate differently in the Carnival. Kenyon, who has earlier accosted the couple wedded by guilt so that the "linked circle of three" forms momentarily a "small circle of isolated feeling," heralds thereby the "small party of soldiers or gendarmes" who arrest both characters and scene. This emblem features his couples confronting each other or the police in the foreground, with a backdrop of costumed multitudes frozen in antic pose.

These emblems, then, illustrate a single character (or couple) at that moment rendered distinct from some symbolic configuration of people. They show isolation succeeding interdependence, serious business succeeding sport. The emblem in *The Scarlet Letter*'s climax conforms to the pattern but the context of the interruption differs. Hawthorne usually writes an outsider breaking in upon festivity and so destroying camaraderie for the major character. In this case an apparent insider breaks out.

The Election Day ceremonies proceed according to plan until Dimmesdale stops the procession at the foot of the scaffold (1:251–52), thus shifting attention from community festivity to personal triumph and tragedy. His funeral march becomes his greatest hour, because his interruption proclaims his control over his own destiny and declares his integrity, which he confirms from the scaffold, site of the public family reunion.

That the character forces the interruption rather than having it forced on him indicates his assuming for himself the task of judgment. Hawthorne allows the character to complete his definition of himself. Dimmesdale stops and steps out in direct contrast to his earlier, private walk from the woods to his rooms, where Mistress Hibbins interrupts his rioting mind. Too, his action contrasts with Hester's passivity in the marketplace spectacle; "statue-like, at the foot of the scaffold," she is interrupted by the witch, the shipmaster, Pearl, and finally the crowd's gaze. Both Dimmesdale and Hester figure in a larger configuration but are not part of it.

By detaching himself and thus altering the day for spectators and readers alike, the character calls our attention to the validity and transience of festivity and its public and private references. The halted procession juxtaposes the public and the private, the social and the personal. One reason to consider these moments of interrupted festivity as emblems is because they hold both references, however contrary, within a single verbal frame. It is time to look more closely at the formal characteristics of these verbal frames so that their identity as a type of emblem is quite clear. Hawthorne borrows, for example, from the masque and sculpture to create a style of allegorical decoration that distinguishes these festive tableaux as emblems.

III

Once writing to his fiancée, Sophia Peabody, Hawthorne remarked:

> I wish there was something in the intellectual world analogous to the Daguerreotype (is that the name of it?) in the visible—something which should print off our deepest, and subtlest, and delicatest thoughts and feelings as minutely and accurately as the above-mentioned instrument paints the various aspects of Nature.[10]

Interruption, which retards the momentum of figures at play, becomes Hawthorne's camera. The momentary stillness between the intact circle and the broken circle "print[s] off" like a snapshot the conflicting truths of community and individuality I have been tracing. Hawthorne's vivid lighting throws into relief the opposition of sport and serious business. The click and flash that record the instant of stillness paradoxically make it endure.

We might recall Motley's comment that the ritual death of Play follows hard upon his brief, brilliant transit in the Roman Carnival. Harlequin's funeral preserves the spirit of his reign, and the flickering torches epitomize its brilliance and transience. Hawthorne detailed in his Notebook the *festa dei moccoletti* or festivity of the little tapers, the traditional concluding ceremony of the Carnival, occurring on the eve of Shrove Tuesday. The phantasmagoria obviously impressed Hawthorne, whose moments of interrupted festivity employ strong colors comparable in visual effect to this scene's chiaroscuro brilliance.

Northrop Frye has written of masques that "The flickering light of candles and torches must have greatly increased the sense of unreality, almost to a point of hallucination."[11] If the

Carnival summarizes the validity of festivity in the romances, its traditional conclusion suggests its transience and the emblematic intent and design of the moments of interruption.[12] Just as Moralities and masques body forth abstractions, so these moments reveal contrary truths, the individual amidst the crowd. The allegorical use of color and dress betrays their intent, and the tableau texture, their design. As emblems, then, they combine the flash of the camera with the coolness of marble; they are brilliant yet enduring.

The survival of the flashing instant in this group of emblems resembles Keats's "Grecian Urn," where verbal art comments upon visual, and both urn and poem happily still life. That poem provides an excellent context for recognizing the design of these emblems. Hawthorne typically prepares the visual allegory of interrupted festivity through his narrator who, like Keats's speaker, enhances the festive tableaux through his commentary. For example, the discourse on the "the forgotten art of gayety" emphasizes "The New England Holiday" tableau in *The Scarlet Letter* (chapter 21), and in *The Marble Faun*, "A Scene in the Corso" (chapter 48) bursts with antic motion in its parts, yet as a whole it feels like a picture.

The slower or faster momentum of festivity gives way to a "lifelessness" in which ideas grow distinct from narrative. Hawthorne explains both the intent and the design of his festive tableaux in such a way that confirms their essential, frozen moments as emblems. He could be describing the intent of all his emblems of interrupted festivity when he writes in *The Scarlet Letter:*

> Nor would it have been impracticable, in the observance of majestic ceremonies, to combine mirthful recreation with solemnity, and give as it were, a grotesque and brilliant embroidery to the great robe of state, which a nation, at such festivals, puts on. [1:230]

He adapts to dress the convention of character names in the Moralities he so loved, with many of his characters wearing variations of Play, Work, Fellowship, Isolation, Guilt, or Evil. Dress becomes a primary mode of definition, and the motley garb befitting scenes of harlequinade discloses a character deliberately and tragically at odds with reality. There is always something of the toy in characters at play. Motley garb advertises the healthiness and exuberance but also the artificiality of play, and in the frozen moment the latter assumes primary importance.

In this context can best be understood *The Scarlet Letter's* "picture of human life in the market-place," which reads like a series of stills anticipating Dimmesdale's halt. His walk back from the forest unleashes his own internal reign of fancy that produces Mistress Hibbins (1:211). Her appearance expresses his illicit sense of imminent freedom; she represents the exotica of evil, a luxuriant bloom of strong contrasts. Hawthorne uses her, the sailors and Indians, the shipmaster, and Pearl similarly to define Hester's unrepentant state. In their color and style of dress, and temporary proximity to Hester, they body forth the couple's temptation, their playful but dangerous avoidance of responsibility. Dimmesdale ironically strides among the bright morions of the procession, as we have noted, since he takes no part in its spirit.

Hawthorne more conspicuously weaves "a grotesque and brilliant embroidery" in his latter two romances to enhance the emblematic intent of their interrupted festivity. In *The Blithedale Romance* the masqueraders wear myriad variations of "the beribboned doublets, silk breeches and stockings, and slippers fastened with artificial roses, that distinguish the pastoral people of poetry and the stage" (3:59). A costumed Westervelt leads the dance, the most calculatedly picturesque and literally fantastic scene in the book, and our eventual view of Zenobia forces us to reconstruct the emblem:

> Zenobia (whose part among the maskers, as may be supposed, was no inferior one) appeared in a costume of fanciful magnificence, with her jewelled flower as the central ornament of what resembled a leafy crown, or coronet. She represented the Oriental princess by whose name we were accustomed to know her. Her attitude was free and noble, yet, if a queen's it was not that of a queen triumphant, but dethroned, on trial for her life, or perchance, condemned already. [3:196–97]

Character has become emblem in this crowning portrait that conflates our experience of the de facto leader of Blithedale; as the center of the circle she is at her most extreme remove from reality.[13] In *The Marble Faun* Hawthorne clothes the international dancers in the Villa Borghese grounds to assess Miriam; their quicksilver presence and absence embodies her temporary exhilaration and futile attempt at repression. The stuffy, self-righteous American in the tableau, condemned for remaining a point outside the circle (4:88), in another respect stands like the reader confronting the emblem.

Later, as authentically apparelled peasant and contadina, Donatello and Miriam play in the Campagna, and in the Carnival she wears a "contadina-costume, of scarlet and gold" (14:502) while both don "an impenetrable black mask." Hilda's "white domino," worn specifically by individuals not impersonating a character, shows her following Carnival tradition (14:440) that has become her own (14:438). With color and costume Hawthorne thus allegorizes innocence and experience, or contrary states of marriage.

Hence, color and dress point out the intent of these emblems and guide our interpretation of them. We confront staged still lifes whose design, I believe, imitates the permanence of painting and sculpture. The texture of these emblems consists not only of costume, but also of pigment and stone. Hawthorne's art, I have said, creates out of these moments of suspended merriment a dynamic interplay of ideas that endures even as details of plot might fade. If the passage on "a grotesque and brilliant embroidery" from *The Scarlet Letter* suggests that intent of these emblems, the Monte Beni banquet-hall in *The Marble Faun* (4:225–26) suggests their design.

These frescoes elaborately depict festivity frozen in the past and subdued by time, and Hawthorne evokes them to serve up his "moral, a grim identity between gay things and sorrowful ones. Only give them a little time, and they turn out to be just alike!"[14] Wall paintings commemorate for the reader the contingency of festivity and display time's leveling influence on interrupted play. In their composition these frescoes represent all of the emblems of interrupted festivity. Hawthorne employs the visual arts to shape these emblems comparable in function to the "brede" in Keats's "Grecian Urn."

The frequent comparisons of the Villa Borghese festivity to marble sculpture is only the clearest example of Hawthorne's emblematic design. In "The Sylvan Dance" and "The Faun and Nymph" (titles of chapters 9 and 10, respectively), Hawthorne shifts to second person in asking us to compare "the wild ring of mirth" with "one of those bas-reliefs" or, more pointedly, "the sculptured scene on the front and sides of a sarcophagus." In other moments of interrupted festivity the analogy is less explicit but nonetheless always present. Hawthorne writes the scenes in such a way that he frames an enduring visual composition. Their emblematic design compares specifically to the organ-grinder's mahogany case in *Seven Gables* discussed earlier.

The contemporary reader of Hawthorne's recurring revels stands in better stead if he studies not only Keats's "Grecian Urn" but also the principles of allegory and the masque. In his study, *The Jonsonian Masque,* Stephen Orgel writes that the masque as a form "attempted from the beginning to breach the barrier between spectators and actors, so that in effect the viewer became part of the spectacle." Further,

> Whatever happens in the masque happens not so much between the characters themselves as between the characters and the viewers. Jonson sees the revels as the moment when the masquer breaks through the limits of his stage, when the illusion moves out into the audience. This is the point toward which the action of the masque moves.[15]

The quintessential moment of the Jonsonian masque compares to the moment of interrupted festivity, just when the momentum of figures at play ceases and their configuration is about to lose its shape. The momentum shifts outward to the reader, who must interpret the emblem of the moment in all its diversity.

Coverdale in Hawthorne's Masque of Modern Arcadia, who slides into its revels between "The Masqueraders" and "Eliot's Pulpit" (titles of chapters 24 and 25, respectively), embodies the reader's task with these emblems. A point outside the circle, he becomes an active witness and interpreter in the foreground, confronting "the suggestive picture" of a "a case of witchcraft." About the Roman Carnival, Hawthorne wrote:

> The scene is quite indescribable, and its effect not to be conceived, without both witnessing and taking part in it. If you merely look at it, it depresses you; if you take even the slightest share in it, you become aware that it has a fascination, and you no longer wonder, at last, that the young people take such delight in plunging into this mad river of fun, that goes roaring through the heart of solemn old Rome, between the narrow limits of the Corso.[14:503–4]

Moments of interrupted festivity constitute a type of emblem prominent in Hawthorne's iconographic style. We savor their richness of composition even as we interpret their interplay of contraries. We take delight in the visual balancing of youthfulness and adulthood, and through our imaginative participation and understanding, we recognize in the type a felicitous example of Hawthorne's power as a romancer.

Notes

1. *The Centenary Edition of the Works of Nathaniel Hawthorne*, ed. William Charvat et al. (Columbus: Ohio State University Press, 1962–), 2 : 163–73. All Hawthorne quotations are from this edition and will be cited by volume and page numbers in the text. For ease of reference, note that the volume numbers for the works cited most often are: 1: *The Scarlet Letter*; 2: *House of the Seven Gables;* 3: *Blithedale Romance;* 4: *Marble Faun;* 14: *French and Italian Notebooks.*

2. Buford Jones traces Hawthorne's adaptation of Spenser's Mammon in his allegorical portrait of the monkey. See "Hawthorne and Spenser: From Allusion to Allegory," in *Nathaniel Hawthorne Journal* (Englewood, Colo.: Microcard Edition Books, 1975), pp. 74–75.

3. These opposed states form the core of at least one book-length study, Arne Axelsson's *Links in the Chain: Isolation and Interdependence in Nathaniel Hawthorne's Fictional Characters* (Stockholm: Rotobeckman, 1974). Axelsson's definition of these ideas provides a helpful thematic context for interpreting interrupted festivity in Hawthorne. He regards interdependence as a positive, reciprocal emotional contact between individuals; isolation represents a breakdown in this contact: "a severing of the links between an individual and the chain of brotherhood is an inner process which is ultimately independent of a person's relations to society" (p. 25).

4. Ibid., p. 28.

5. Hawthorne later uses the young Italian organ-grinder again to compare, this time with mordant effect, the individual isolated from a blithe group. The company of dancing toys mirrors the swirl of children around the organ-grinder when Hawthorne hauls him back onto Pyncheon Street to serenade the dead Joffrey Pyncheon, entombed within the House (2 : 293 ff.). Again, the minor character and his fanciful show exist to point the moral.

6. John Huizinga discusses the sanctity and validity of a community's "playground." See *Homo Ludens: A Study of the Play Element in Culture* (Boston: Beacon Press, 1955), pp. 10–11, 19–21.

7. Albert D. Blissert, "The Function of Play and Possession in the Works of Nathaniel Hawthorne" (Ph. D. diss., Johns Hopkins University, 1976), *DIA:* 2177A.

8. The tableau certainly helped Richard Chase to conclude, *"The Scarlet Letter* is almost all picture . . . [the dramatic scenes of the novel] are like the events in a pageant . . . they have the effect of being observed by the reader at second hand, of being reported to him, as in 'picture.'" See *The American Novel and Its Tradition* (Garden City, N.Y.: Doubleday, 1957), p. 70.

9. John C. Stubbs concludes similarly. He believes that their play is unreal—that their forest dance is a game as is their whole enterprise—and also that their play reveals "their emotional selves," "their basic humanness." Their play is thus both unreal and emotionally real, and I have been arguing that this seeming contradiction is true to the tableaux. See *The Pursuit of Form: A Study of Hawthorne and the Romance* (Urbana: University of Illinois Press, 1970), p. 135.

10. *Love Letters,* quoted by Marjorie J. Elder in *Nathaniel Hawthorne: Transcendental Symbolist* (Athens: Ohio University Press, 1969), p. 75. French psychologist Jean Normand speculates about Hawthorne's attraction to the daguerreotype, which he likens to the movie screen. He thinks Hawthorne's pictorial disposition is insistently cinematic, while I do not. See the section titled "The Diorama" in *An Approach to an Analysis of Artistic Creation,* trans. Derek Coltman (Cleveland, Ohio: Case Western University Press, 1970), pp. 308–33.

11. Frye writes, "Like a miniature World's Fair, where a whole city is set up and torn down, the masque was an enormously expensive and variegated performance which glittered for a night and disappeared . . . 'These things are but toys,' is Bacon's opening remark in his essay, and the masque does have something of the cultural quality that Fabergé symbolized in a later age, of elaborate 'devices' or playthings for a leisure class." Northrop Frye, *Spiritus Mundi* (Bloomington: Indiana University Press, 1976), p. 158.

12. During the *festa,* participants would engage in a mock battle, trying to blow out others' *moccoli* and preserve their own. The phantasmagoria obviously impressed Hawthorne who, when most of the torches were extinguished and the lesser gas-lights shone forth, typically moralized about the latter: "They were what the fixed stars are to the transitory splendors of human life" (14:504). The relationship of torches to gas-lights recapitulates the relationship of sport to serious business, and play to work. It also illustrates the fusion of theme and form in this group of emblems.

13. Patricia Carlson interprets the picture in terms of character and fits it with the romance's earlier self-defining stage appearances of Zenobia: by this point, she "has denied reality and wholly transformed herself into the delusion of the 'role' she has been impersonating." See *Hawthorne's Functional Settings* (Amsterdam: Rodopi, 1977), p. 35.

14. Hawthorne adapted the moralizing gloss for the banquet-hall almost verbatim from his Notebook. While visiting the Florentine church of Santa Croce, he discerned in the "horrible frescoes by Giotto, Cimabue, or their compeers" a "new shade of human misery": "these frescoes are to a church what dreary, old remembrances are to a mind" (14:344–45).

15. Stephen Orgel, *The Jonsonian Masque* (Cambridge: Harvard University Press, 1965), p. 198. Orgel informs us that the revels, or dance, traditionally concluded a masque. Coverdale, of course, witnesses and then eludes an anti-masque, before the Eliot's Pulpit conclusion. Orgel writes, "the anti-masque world was a world of particularity and mutability—of accidents; the masque world was one of ideal abstractions and eternal verities" (p. 73). But by the early seventeenth century, the anti-masque assumed an increasingly larger role and in effect stole the show: "the world of accidents began to overshadow the world of essence" (p. 73). Hawthorne in his dance scenes seems to graft the form and tone of the anti-masque onto the purpose and place of the masque.

"Far and Momentary Glimpses": Hawthorne's Treatment of Mrs. Wakefield

Laura Laffrado

SUNY at Buffalo

MODERN criticism of Hawthorne's "Wakefield" concentrates on Wakefield himself, his urban surroundings, and Hawthorne as cultural analyst.[1] Little of the spotlight is devoted to Mrs. Wakefield, who still lurks outside the pale beam of criticism—stout, retiring, and very likely misunderstood. The general conclusion is that Mrs. Wakefield is dormant after the disappearance of her husband, "resigned to her autumnal widowhood,"[2] and that she lapses into a sorrowful and dull life until Wakefield returns twenty years later. Borges, in his criticism, follows this pattern, never questioning the surface information Hawthorne has given us about Mrs. Wakefield.[3] Roberta Weldon, looking more closely, suggests that at the story's end Wakefield has remade his wife in his image and that this alteration accounts for the remarkable activity of her shadow as she sits by the fireside.[4]

Such readings tend to view Mrs. Wakefield peripherally while focusing on Mr. Wakefield. He has left; she has remained; and as the source of action in the story, he is followed. I suggest that Mrs. Wakefield has action of her own in the story: that she gains her freedom by her husband's departure and that her very presence as a component of matrimony and of love in the story makes her a major element in fully understanding "Wakefield."

34

A close examination of Hawthorne's description of her shadow on the wall at the story's end reveals that far from being a projection from Wakefield onto his wife, the shadow is in reality a reflection of the power granted to Mrs. Wakefield by her husband's disappearance. Her shadow should indeed appear exaggerated and too merry: she has been awarded liberty, a condition received by too few women of the nineteenth century. For twenty years she has been able to determine her own life. As a widow, mourning but not devastated by the lapse of a passionless marriage, financially independent, she controls her own life. No wonder Wakefield pauses when he sees her significant shadow, no wonder Hawthorne breaks narrative tone and warns Wakefield not to enter. A closer look will show that a woman once set free and allowed time to adjust to her new life may still "keep carefully the gray coat and small-clothes in the closet of their bed chamber" (p. 80), but will never run to fetch them as she would have twenty years earlier. She, too, has undergone a great change.

A careful look at Hawthorne's language in "Wakefield" reveals that he wished to emphasize matrimony as a major element of this fourteen-paragraph story. Hawthorne begins immediately. "In some old magazine or newspaper I recollect a story, told as truth, of a man—let us call him Wakefield—who absented himself for a long time from his wife" (p. 75). In this first sentence, "man" and "wife" are set up as a pair, indicating both alienation (only Mrs. Wakefield is described as a spouse) and invoking tones of the marriage ceremony. Hawthorne as narrator rushes in to soothe us before the first line of the story can cause alarm: leaving one's wife is not uncommon, he tells us, and besides, this is an odd tale, certainly not a common occurrence. The narrator will continue this soothing throughout the story, but in the meantime "wedded couple," "man / wife," "matrimonial felicity," and "loving spouse," continue to sprout up in the first paragraph. These language clues, threaded throughout the first seven sentences, lead directly to the conclusion that Wakefield could not leave just anyone he happened to be living with; the story would not function the same if he left his mother. He must, for Hawthorne's full meaning to be revealed, leave his wife, and these many references draw our attention to the importance of the wife right from the start.

Yet we have a fickle narrator at work here. Though he wishes to alert us to matrimony as an integral element in the story, he will not favor us with obvious references. Instead, his ironic tone, coupled with some interesting sentence structure, tries to lure the unsuspecting reader away from the actual meaning of what is written:

> And after so great a gap in his matrimonial felicity—when his death was reckoned certain, his estate settled, his name dismissed from memory, and his wife, long, long ago, resigned to her autumnal widowhood—he entered the door one evening, quietly, as from a day's absence, and became a loving spouse till death. [P. 75]

Bombarded as we are with information in this sentence, including the end of the story, one is tempted to take it for what it is worth and continue reading. But what is the information worth? Are we to accept these phrases as truth, delivered by a straight-forward narrator? I do not believe it. The use of "matrimonial felicity" seems to indicate that the narrator's tongue is firmly in cheek: we have been given no impression that any sort of felicity exists in this marriage. Were an ironic tone to be applied to this sentence then, the value of the given facts becomes doubtful. They, too, could be meant as exaggerations of the truth. "His name dismissed from memory," a traditional Chinese method of punishing those who have disgraced their families, suddenly becomes suspicious as serious wording, along with "long, long ago" chiming fairy-tale notes in the background. Finally, this sentence that seems to sum up the entire story ends on the word "death." Such an ending not only casts into doubt the happiness of the reunion, but indicates that our narrator is a slippery fellow who does not always mean what he appears to be saying. The ultimate effect of such language is the knowledge that each sentence of "Wakefield" (and indeed of all of Hawthorne's fiction) must be firmly gripped and then examined word by word in context before any conclusion can be drawn.

Before Wakefield is allowed to leave his wife, the narrator describes the character of the man who will be absent from her side:

> his matrimonial affections, never violent, were sobered into a calm, habitual sentiment; of all husbands, he was likely to be the most constant, because a certain sluggishness would keep his heart at rest, wherever it might be placed. [P. 75]

This description leaves us to conjecture that Mr. Wakefield, though "constant," had few of the virtues of a truly loving spouse. The use of "sluggishness" not only reveals the presence of the narrator's distinctive tone, but leads us to question exactly what it is that Mrs. Wakefield is going to miss when her husband disappears.

As Mr. Wakefield "informs" his wife that he will be away, she is "indulgent" (p. 76), the first direct indication that she is more observant than he, both in terms of understanding his personality and tolerating his odd habits. Wakefield is referred to as her "husband" here for the first time: the last time she sees him is the first time he is called this. He then smiles his way out of the paragraph, leaving the narrator to muse on Mrs. Wakefield's interpretations of that smile.

But unlike Wakefield, we are not allowed to leave the paragraph so quickly. "But our business is with the husband," the fifth paragraph begins, surely a line meant to send us straight back to the fourth paragraph. Had Hawthorne ended paragraph four with that line, we would have mentally indented and begun to follow Wakefield, too. To begin the following paragraph with this, however, suggests that the meaning of the sentence should be considered: that part of our business is indeed with Mrs. Wakefield and with her reactions to her husband's departure. Again, a language clue has been left for us to follow, as the narrator concentrates briefly on Mrs. Wakefield, and then interrupts himself to insist that "our business is with the husband." This is just enough to make the careful reader uneasy as to with whom our business really is, protestations of the narrator notwithstanding.

"Chaste bosom," "thy true wife," "good Mrs. Wakefield," and "exemplary wife" all function as descriptions of Mrs. Wakefield. But who is it that sees her this way? Perhaps the narrator's ironic tone is at work or perhaps this is Mrs. Wakefield seen through the eyes of her husband. She is also labeled as a "widow of a week" here, long before Wakefield is assumed dead by anyone. Their relationship was such that she was near widowhood before he ever left, taking his sluggish emotions with him.

Once Mrs. Wakefield realizes that her spouse is gone, we are again presented with a winding sentence by our narrator. "In the course of a few weeks she gradually recovers; the crisis is over; her heart is sad, perhaps, but quiet" (p. 78). And again, we must look closely to determine what is meant. "Perhaps" can operate two ways here: as a hinge between "sad" and "quiet," linking the two, or as an element of doubt as to whether her heart is really sad at all, surely a strange suggestion to make about a "forlorn widow."

Wakefield seems more forlorn than his wife, since he is faithful to her, while "he is slowly fading out" of her heart (p. 78). Mrs. Wakefield then, presumably, moves into the future, recovering from her husband's supposed death, while Mr. Wakefield remains in the past, his emotions, such as they are, remaining constant to her. Her recovery from the lack of her spouse allows her to endure in her new life and ten years pass.

For the first time in a decade, we look closely at Mrs. Wakefield. She is portly, older, placid, and "her regrets have either died away, or . . ." (p. 79). Or? We are given a choice here by Hawthorne, a choice easily overlooked given the rest of that sentence: "or have become so essential to her heart, that they would be poorly exchanged for joy." The description of Mrs. Wakefield and the latter half of the sentence so sandwich the idea that her regrets may have completely died away that only the careful reader will understand one choice that may indeed be made is that Mrs. Wakefield has no regrets concerning her husband, which certainly does not make her a forlorn widow still yearning for the presence of her spouse. In this context, "portly," "placid mien," and "well-conditioned," do not carry negative connotations. Thus, we are not forced to accept that Mrs. Wakefield's regrets would be necessarily "poorly exchanged for joy," and we are also not forced to view Mrs. Wakefield as the archetypal widow. Recovered from her regrets, participating in the community at least through church-going, she has taken a giant step away from the wife she once was.

When Mrs. Wakefield bumps into her husband in the twelfth paragraph, she glances back, perplexed by this meeting, as well she should be. Her perplexed feelings stem from the fact that she should feel something, though she doesn't know what or why. Her marriage operated in much the same way: we recall that she met Mr. Wakefield's "parting kiss in the matter-of-course way of a ten years' matrimony" (p. 76). Another ten years have passed and her emotions concerning Wakefield have weakened to the point of nonrecognition.

After this meeting, the narrator says of Wakefield, "he was, we may figuratively say, always beside his wife and at his hearth, yet must never feel the warmth of the one nor the affection of the other" (p. 79). Mrs. Wakefield is linked in the narrator's language with an inanimate object and thus becomes another symbol of the home. This impression is bolstered when the narrator exclaims, "Alas, what a mistake!" (p. 79) when Wakefield imagines that his wife would "clap her hands for joy" (p. 79) were he to reappear. Wakefield is unable to reinterpret his wife's emotions and reactions correctly. Like Robin in "My Kinsman, Major Molineux," he is outside the community and is unable to interpret signs correctly, becoming a latter-day Rip Van Winkle through his long absence from common custom.

As Wakefield stands in the rain yet another decade later, Hawthorne's language takes a curious turn. Mrs. Wakefield is, once again, "the good Mrs. Wakefield" (p. 80); the word "autumnal" makes a reappearance (p. 80), this time not in reference to widowhood but to a chill seizing Wakefield. And "Shall he stand, wet and shivering here, when his own hearth has a good fire to warm him, and his own wife" (p. 80) introduces the reappearance of the hearth and wife pair seen earlier. With these three repetitions in the penultimate paragraph, Hawthorne is shooting fireworks off the page. Such repetition, all in reference to Mrs. Wakefield, cannot be accidental. She is essential not only in this scene, but in the entire story. If these repetitions lead us to concentrate more on Mrs. Wakefield, in what direction does our concentration take us? Undoubtedly, we move toward her reaction to Mr. Wakefield's return. It is this movement that makes "Wakefield" a precursor of sorts of the modern, open-ended short story, with Mrs. Wakefield's reaction being the pivot on which the ending turns.

Finally, with "doubtless," "at his wife's expense," and "quizzed" (p. 80), the narrator returns to his ironic tone and speaks of "the happy event—supposing it to be such" (p. 80), and thus again tries to lead the reader off the page and away from the most serious implications of "Wakefield."

What Hawthorne presents us with, then, is a series of language clues indicating that to understand the story fully we must look to Mrs. Wakefield. And to look fully at Mrs. Wakefield, we must glance briefly at the nineteenth-century married woman. In *Commentaries of the Laws of England* Sir William Blackstone states:

> The husband and wife are one person in law; that is, the very being or legal existence of the woman is suspended during the marriage,

or at least is incorporated and consolidated into that of the husband: under whose wing, protection and cover, she performs everything.[5]

The legal status of women, regardless of class, was dismal at best, and few women found themselves in a position of independence and financial comfort. A great deal of discussion and writing in the eighteenth and nineteenth centuries was devoted to rights for women and keeping rights from women. Mary Wollstonecraft's *Vindication of the Rights of Woman* (1792) not only makes clear how women were deprived, but also reveals the popularity of works concerning women's attitudes. She finds no shortage of works to take to task for their representations of women.[6] Both Mary Ann Radcliffe's *The Female Advocate* (1799) and Priscilla Wakefield's *Reflections on the present condition of the female sex; with suggestions for its improvement* (1798) provide sociological evidence for the fettered and unhappy condition of women of the time.

"Gender and Genre: Women in British Romantic Literature," an essay by Irene Tayler and Gina Luria, reveals that this viewpoint was not only being discussed and written about in nonfiction, but was becoming a major subject for extrapolation in the novel:

> Novels abound with illegitimate births, consenting seductions, filial rebellions, economic worries, even expressions of feelings as mundane as boredom. Set against this welter of the actual is the suggestion of a new ideal: a strong young woman who can define the values that determine her fate and make them stick.[7]

In short, numerous examples existed concerning this subject and Hawthorne would certainly have realized that some women had a great deal to gain by their husbands' disappearing, to leave them unhampered by children and financially secure. Later treatment of Hester Prynne suggests that a pre-Sophia Hawthorne had at least the seeds of sensibility and sensitivity regarding men, women, and marriage. Yet with her widowhood, her outwardly static life after Wakefield leaves, her presence at the home hearth when he chooses to return, it is tempting to accept Mrs. Wakefield as a device, a stock character. If she is indeed meant to be an archetypal widow, it is necessary to look at Hawthorne's modifications of that type.

Her quick recovery after Wakefield's supposed death, a limited mourning period, and brief illness, leave our widow open to the charge of near-indifference to her husband's absence. Though she may not be gleeful, Mrs. Wakefield remains basically unchanged after her husband relocates. John Gatta has suggested that "the basic superficiality of Wakefield's relationship to his wife even apart from their current bodily separation"[8] is revealed when the two meet on the street. Why not extend this to include Mrs. Wakefield's reaction throughout her husband's absence? It is her lack of a reaction that associates her with Gatta's notion on the use of London as the setting for "Wakefield": "Here one finds Hawthorne's darkest meditation on the anomic terrors and threats to interior selfhood posed by an age of rapid urban expansion."[9] Wakefield's ability to approach his home without being taken notice of by "busy and selfish London" (p. 79) corresponds with his approaching his wife just as safely. Mrs. Wakefield then, in a certain sense, can serve as a mirror of the city, in that she is nearly as indifferent and seemingly just as unchanged after her husband's disappearance. Strength of character and strength of relationship are needed to survive the vastly impersonal world of the city; both are absent from the Wakefields long before Mr. Wakefield leaves home. Without these strengths, one's strongest bonds are weak indeed, and it is fairly easy for one's wife to carry on, busy and selfish, without one.

Mrs. Wakefield could also represent a domestic object for Wakefield. Along with the fire in the hearth and the clothes in the closet, she may be another prop of home life, inactive and gathering dust until Wakefield returns. Wakefield does think of her in this connection—"Shall he stand, wet and shivering here, when his own hearth has a good fire to warm him, and his own wife will run to fetch the gray coat" (p. 80)—and she is representative of the home life he left behind.

Both interpretations of Mrs. Wakefield, as an extension of the impersonality of London and as a cardboard cutout in the window, weaken when faced with Hawthorne's most striking addition to the archetypal widow. Mrs. Wakefield's active and exaggerated shadow at the story's end, no matter what interpretation is assigned to it, is an image of power:

On the ceiling appears a grotesque shadow of good Mrs. Wakefield. The cap, the nose and chin, and the broad waist, form an admirable caricature, which dances, moreover, with up-flickering and down-

sinking blaze, almost too merrily for the shade of an elderly widow.
[P. 80]

Where this power will go once Wakefield walks in the door is
unknown to us; but when we last see her, Mrs. Wakefield is a
powerful image, too powerful, in fact, to be a stock character.
Weldon argues that the wall shadow is Mrs. Wakefield transformed into the angular and phallic Mr. Wakefield of the street
meeting ten years earlier, that it is Wakefield's "altered perception" that causes her shadow to behave so oddly.[10] According to
Weldon, "He has imposed his identity upon her instead of
reconciling himself to what she represents."[11] Yet if Mrs.
Wakefield merits the attention that Hawthorne has paid her in
language throughout the story, why must this power come to
her secondhand? The "admirable caricature" dancing "almost
too merrily for the shade of an elderly widow" is indeed angular and phallic, but what better way to present the ster-
eotypical qualities of a man, the very masculine power in which
twenty years of independence has resulted? It is this power that
Hawthorne cautions against as Wakefield stands in the rain.
The infusion of power into a passionless relationship should
indeed cause him to pause.

Mrs. Wakefield, then, can perhaps function as an extension
of Mr. Wakefield, reacting but never acting as Weldon maintains, her power coming only from her husband. His action,
performed the night he stayed away, has led him through
twenty years of a hollow and fairly mad life in London. Her
reaction has allowed her freedom from mourning, release from
a sluggish marriage, and a quiet life of independence. A stock
character, perhaps, but one with disturbing and unusual modifications.

So we now see Mrs. Wakefield step into the spotlight she has
avoided for so long. The woman seen after careful study is not
only portly and in the wane of her life. She is an unremarkable
woman who chose poorly when she married and, after her
husband's departure, seems related to the twentieth-century
urban woman who, abandoned or divorced, carries on in virtual isolation within a crowd. Mrs. Wakefield would be as lost as
her husband in London, but, unlike him, she does not step
outside the established boundaries. Once she has gained her
freedom, though she takes no active steps to do so, she spends it
more prudently than does Wakefield. A man without inner

resources to draw on, the most he can do during his journey is to observe the past. Indeed, twenty years after he left home he still thinks of putting on his old clothes, clothes that will fit him no better than the world from which he is outcast. Though Mrs. Wakefield may also think of the past, she uses her freedom to remain in touch with the community, thus remaining in touch with the world.

Finally, this seems to be a story that has a great deal to do with love. If the Wakefields had had a loving marriage, Mr. Wakefield would not have left. It would not have been so easy for him to get lost inside himself, not to mention getting lost in London. Wakefield's ability to leave home so casually, Mrs. Wakefield's ability to carry on without him, and their unimaginative and mechanical reactions once they gain their freedom, reveal two people who lack the substance that will anchor them firmly together in society. In order to resist the impersonality of urban sprawl, to resist the progress that makes it too easy to become lost in the crowd and separated from one's self, one needs love. Without love, Wakefield is free to leave home and become lost forever. Without love, Mrs. Wakefield can remain a part of the community, but still be cut off from human contact and thus exist on the outer limits of the community. "Wakefield" then becomes a romance in reverse, revealing the dangers of thoughtless drifting away from the community, away from the essential heart of a human relationship, into the loveless universe.

Notes

1. Studies focusing on Hawthorne's "Wakefield" include: Thomas F. Walsh, Jr., "'Wakefield' and Hawthorne's Illustrated Ideas: A Study in Form," *Emerson Society Quarterly*, No. 25 (1961), pp. 29–35; John Gatta, Jr., "'Busy and Selfish London': The Urban Figure in Hawthorne's 'Wakefield,'" *Emerson Society Quarterly* 23, no. 3 (1977): 164–72; and Andrew Schiller, "The Moment and the Endless Voyage: A Study of Hawthorne's 'Wakefield,'" *Diameter* 1 (1951): 7–12.

2. *The Complete Short Stories of Nathaniel Hawthorne* (Garden City, N.Y.: Doubleday, 1959), p. 75; subsequent page numbers appear in parentheses in the text.

3. Jorge Luis Borges, *Other Inquisitions, 1937–1952* (Austin: University of Texas Press, 1964), pp. 47–65.

4. Roberta F. Weldon, "Wakefield's Second Journey," *Studies in Short Fiction* 14 (1977): 69–74.

5. Sir William Blackstone, *Commentaries of the Laws of England, Book the First* (Oxford, 1765), p. 442.

6. Mary Wollstonecraft, *A Vindication of the Rights of Woman* (Farnborough: Gregg, 1970), pp. 170–258.

7. Irene Tayler and Gina Luria, "Gender and Genre: Women in British Romantic Literature," in *What Manner of Woman: Essays on English and American Life and Literature,* ed. Marlene Springer (New York: New York University Press, 1977), p. 110.

8. Gatta, "'Busy and Selfish London,'" pp. 168–69.

9. Ibid., p. 164.

10. Weldon, "Wakefield's Second Journey," p. 73.

11. Ibid., p. 74.

Baby Chillingworth: Hawthorne's Use of Heredity in *The Scarlet Letter*

Ronald Emerick

Indiana University of Pennsylvania

NATHANIEL Hawthorne traces the effects of heredity in several of his tales and novels. Frequently a child inherits the dominant traits of his parents' personalities, and he may also inherit outstanding physical, moral, or spiritual characteristics. In "The Gentle Boy" Ilbrahim's religion and his heavenly nature are instinctive; he has inherited them from his parents rather than learned them from indoctrination in the Quaker faith. Similarly, in "The Artist of the Beautiful" Robert Danforth's son, with a certain odd and shrewd expression on his face, shows his grandfather's skepticism and mockery as he smashes Owen Warland's butterfly in his hand.

All of Hawthorne's romances reveal the influence of heredity in major characters. Not only physical but also moral and supernatural traits are inherited by the Pyncheons and the Maules in *The House of the Seven Gables*. Several of the Pyncheons inherit their ancestor's evil nature and a curse in the form of reappearing apoplexy, and the Maules inherit a vengeful disposition and the power of psychological dominance through hypnosis. In *The Blithedale Romance* the difference between Zenobia and Priscilla is also attributed to heredity. Both women have the same father but exhibit strikingly different personalities because of the circumstances of their birth. Zenobia is the proud daughter of Fauntleroy's happy and successful first marriage, while shy Priscilla is the product of the disgraced Fauntleroy and his meek second wife. And Donatello, that fantastic creature from *The Marble Faun,* inherits his carefree, fawnlike nature (and perhaps even pointed, furry ears) from generations of similar semi-human beings.

Hawthorne also emphasizes heredity in the portrayal of Pearl in *The Scarlet Letter.* As Ernest Sandeen points out, she is a product of sin and "an incarnation of the passion which gave her birth; a living scarlet letter, she is wild, whimsical, willful, irresponsible, and full of strong anti-social feelings."[1] In remarks by various characters throughout the novel, Hawthorne implies that Pearl bears the stamp of both of her parents. When Hester takes Pearl to Governor Bellingham's mansion to plead for a mother's rights, Roger Chillingworth suggests the theory of heredity as a key to Pearl's parentage:

"A strange child!" remarked old Roger Chillingworth. "It is easy to see the mother's part in her. Would it be beyond a philosopher's research, think ye, gentlemen, to analyze that child's nature, and, from its make and mould, to give a shrewd guess at the father?"[2]

Similarly, in the forest scene in chapter 19 Hester and Dimmesdale discuss Pearl's physical heredity:

"She is a splendid child! But I know whose brow she has!"

"Dost thou know, Hester," said Arthur Dimmesdale, with an unquiet smile, "that this dear child, tripping about always at thy side, hath caused me many an alarm. Methought—O Hester, what a thought is that, and how terrible to dread it!—that my own features were partly repeated in her face, and so strikingly that the world might see them! But she is mostly thine!"

"No, no! Not mostly!" answered the mother, with a tender smile. "A little longer, and thou needest not to be afraid to trace whose child she is." [P. 206]

As if to confirm Hester's statement about heredity, Hawthorne adds:

In her was visible the tie that united them. She had been offered to the world, these seven years past, as the living hieroglyphic, in which was revealed the secret they so darkly sought to hide,—all written in this symbol,—all plainly manifest,—had there been a prophet or magician skilled to read the character of flame! [Pp. 206–7]

Thus, both Hawthorne and his characters suggest that Pearl has inherited traits from both her father and mother. Although Pearl's inheritance from Hester is clearly revealed in the novel, her inheritance from Dimmesdale is not so obvious. Despite Seymour Katz's claim that "Pearl's initial being is obviously derived from Hester's and Dimmesdale's natures by a principle of genetic probabilities,"[3] it appears that Pearl hasn't inherited anything from Dimmesdale but a brow. There is so little similarity in their personalities and character traits that any of the other male characters in *The Scarlet Letter* could just as easily be Pearl's father, because they show just as much resemblance to her as Dimmesdale. In fact one of them—Roger Chillingworth—is so like Pearl in the outstanding features of his character that, if the details of the novel didn't prohibit it, it would be tempting to claim that Hester Prynne and Roger Chillingworth, rather than Hester Prynne and Arthur Dimmesdale, were the true parents of little Pearl.

Hawthorne lays a solid foundation for Hester as Pearl's mother, for their characters are similar in many respects. Both possess natural grace and native energy; both exhibit courage, tenderness, and imagination; and both are characterized as unusually passionate and defiant. Hester's natural dignity and force of character are seen in her first appearance in the novel as she steps from the prison into the sunlight:

> The young woman was tall, with a figure of perfect elegance, on a large scale. She had dark and abundant hair, so glossy that it threw off the sunshine with a gleam, and a face which, besides being beautiful from regularity of feature and richness of complexion, had the impressiveness belonging to a marked brow and deep black eyes. She was lady-like, too, after the manner of the feminine gentility of those days; characterized by a certain state and dignity, rather than by the delicate, evanescent, and indescribable grace, which is now recognized as its indication. [P. 53]

But her grace is fortified in this scene by energy, courage, pride, and defiance. As Terence Martin points out, to bear her ordeal she "dons an armor of pride" and "undeniably . . . flaunts the letter."[4] She has sinned against society's law, but not against her own passionate nature; therefore she is not truly contrite.[5] This same courage and pride are seen in her conduct under the accusing gazes of her fellow citizens, and in her trying meetings with Chillingworth and Dimmesdale. Fostered by enforced isolation, her defiant attitude breeds an independent spirit and a revolutionary mind.

The same natural grace and energy are apparent in little Pearl:

> Certainly, there was no physical defect. By its perfect shape, its vigor, and its natural dexterity in the use of all its untried limbs, the infant was worthy to have been brought forth in Eden; worthy to have been left there, to be the plaything of the angels, after the world's first parents were driven out. The child had a native grace which does not invariably coexist with faultless beauty. [P. 90]

Hawthorne also notes Pearl's unflagging vivacity of spirits; she is always in motion, a virtual dynamo of activity:

> It was wonderful, the vast variety of forms into which she threw her intellect, with no continuity, indeed, but darting and dancing, always in a state of preternatural activity,—soon sinking down, as if exhausted by so rapid and feverish a tide of life,—and succeeded by other shapes of similar wild energy. [P. 95]

Hester also observes her own passionate nature and proud defiance in Pearl. The child obeys her mother only when she wants to. When her mother tries to quiet her at Governor Bellingham's mansion, Pearl emits one of her eldritch shrieks before becoming silent. During the forest scene when Hester asks her to leap across the brook, she breaks into a fit of wild shrieks and contortions and refuses to budge. She likewise refuses to bestow favors upon Dimmesdale simply because Hester asks her to.

In order to explain Pearl's passionate and defiant nature, Hester blames herself and the ordeal she underwent during her pregnancy: "Above all, the warfare of Hester's spirit at that epoch, was perpetuated in Pearl. She could recognize her wild, desperate, defiant mood, the flightiness of her temper, and even some of the very cloud-shapes of gloom and despondency that had brooded in her heart" (p. 91). Hawthorne echoes Hester's explanation when he adds: "All this enmity and passion had Pearl inherited, by inalienable right, out of Hester's heart. . . . and in the nature of the child seemed to be perpetuated those unquiet elements that had distracted Hester Prynne before Pearl's birth" (pp. 94–95). Barbara Garlitz confirms Hawthorne's accuracy in relating Pearl's perversity and defiance to her mother's mental agony: "In making Pearl a microcosm of Hester's moral chaos, Hawthorne was not merely creating an elaborate symbol for the scarlet letter; he was also describing a real child in terms of the current physiological psychology, which offered him a means of natural symbolism."[6]

But Pearl has inherited more than her mother's bold and harsh traits; she has also inherited the softer, more feminine attributes of tenderness and imagination. Hester's tenderness is obvious in her kind treatment of Pearl and Dimmesdale as well as her constant deeds of charity to her fellow citizens: "Hester's nature showed itself warm and rich; a well-spring of human tenderness, unfailing to every real demand, and inexhaustible by the largest" (p. 161). Her ingenuity with a needle and thread reveals her unusual imagination. Although she puts this imagination to practical use as a seamstress for the village, she also uses it to create the skillful embroidery of the scarlet letter and Pearl's fantastic clothing.

Pearl reflects her mother's imagination in her ability to create her own playmates and playthings:

> The spell of life went forth from her ever creative spirit, and communicated itself to a thousand objects, as a torch kindles a flame wherever it may be applied. The unlikeliest materials, a stick, a bunch of rags, a flower, were the puppets of Pearl's witchcraft, and, without undergoing any outward change, became spiritually adapted to whatever drama occupied the stage of her inner world. [P. 95]

Whether playing at home, by the seashore, or in the forest, she is never idle because of her active, creative mind. She has even "inherited her mother's gift for devising drapery and costume" (p. 178) and can fashion a green "scarlet letter" of her own.

In the scene at Bellingham's mansion when Dimmesdale pleads for Hester's right to her daughter, Pearl's reaction shows that Hester's love and tenderness are also exquisitely developed in her: "Pearl, that wild and flighty little elf, stole softly towards him, and, taking his hand in the grasp of both her own, laid her cheek against it; a caress so tender, and withal so unobtrusive, that her mother, who was looking on, asked herself,—'Is that my Pearl?'" (p. 115). Similarly, during the forest scene, "in a mood of tenderness that was not unusual with her, she drew down her mother's head, and kissed her brow and both her cheeks" (p. 211) after Hester replaced the discarded scarlet letter on her breast.

Although Pearl has obviously inherited many traits from her mother, she has inherited little or nothing from her father. A short list of the outstanding characteristics of Dimmesdale's personality reveals no similarities to Pearl's. He is sensitive, sympathetic, weak willed, cowardly, morbid, masochistic, and hypocritical. His religious sensibility and persuasive voice and manner are counterbalanced by an exceedingly nervous temperament, an oversensitive conscience, and a passionate, somewhat animalistic nature. His hypersensitive conscience and lack of strength make him an easy target for Chillingworth's attack. By carefully prodding Dimmesdale's weaknesses of character, Chillingworth causes him to be overcome and practically destroyed by his own flaws. In the forest scene near the end of the novel Dimmesdale has become so weak and uncertain that he must depend upon Hester's strength to sustain him and make his decisions for him. It is probably only this second encounter with temptation and his realization that he can never escape his conscience which give him the strength to make his public confession. Dimmesdale has also discovered that by permitting himself to commit one sin, he risks losing all his inhibitions and allowing himself to succumb to many other sins.[7]

Clearly, Pearl's character reveals little influence from her father's traits. The only similarity between these two characters would seem to be their sensitivity; however, Dimmesdale's is a moral and spiritual sensitivity, whereas Pearl's is an intuitive perception of truth. If Pearl is an amoral creature, she perceives only truth, not morality. The fact that she acts as a moral agent in her perception of truth does not necessarily prove that she has inherited any moral awareness. Although Darrel Abel claims that Pearl has been influenced by both of her parents—"Pearl thus mirrored her parents' proclivities because the germ of infant life is the fruit of the mature lives which engendered it"[8]—he gives no real proof of any inheritance from her father. Rather he bases his theory on Pearl's moral function in the novel as a prick to her parents' consciences. However, we must not confuse Pearl's perception of truth with moral awareness.

Although none of Pearl's character traits are like her father's, two of her outstanding traits are similar to two of Roger Chillingworth's main characteristics. Both have an intuitive, almost uncanny perception of truth, and both are described as perverse, diabolic tormentors.

Roger Chillingworth's skill as a truth-seeker is unquestionable. His life of study and meditation, his dabbling in alchemy, and his experience with Indian practices and superstitions have fostered an acute intelligence and exceptional skills in reasoning: "There was a remarkable intelligence in his features, as of a person who had so cultivated his mental part that it could not fail to mould the physical to itself, and become manifest by unmistakable tokens" (p. 60). Even Dimmesdale recognizes in him "an intellectual cultivation of no moderate depth or scope" (p. 123). In fact, he has cultivated his intelligence so thoroughly that he is even capable of reading the human soul. He can easily ferret out the guilt and shame of a tortured soul like Dimmesdale's. Therefore, he immediately recognizes the mystery of Pearl's father as an apt subject for his mental capacities and readily accepts the problem as a challenge to his skill.

But there is more to Chillingworth's awareness than just an acute intelligence. As Hawthorne says, he possessed "native sagacity, and a nameless something more,—let us call it intuition" (p. 124). It is this nameless something extra, this intuitive perception of Chillingworth's, combined with his intelligence, which enables him to so easily discover the truth about Dimmesdale. As he so confidently tells Hester during his interview with her in the prison:

> "Never know him! Believe me, Hester, there are few things,— whether in the outward world, or, to a certain depth, in the invisible sphere of thought,—few things hidden from the man, who devotes himself earnestly and unreservedly to the solution of a mystery. Thou mayest cover up thy secret from the prying multitude. Thou mayst conceal it, too, from the ministers and magistrates, even as thou didst this day, when they sought to wrench the name out of thy heart, and give thee a partner on thy pedestal. But, as for me, I come to the inquest with other senses than they possess. I shall seek this man, as I have sought truth in books; as I have sought gold in alchemy. There is a sympathy that will make me conscious of him. I shall see him tremble. I shall feel myself shudder, suddenly and unawares. Sooner or later, he must needs be mine!" [P. 75]

Armed with his intelligence and intuition, Chillingworth exhibits the skill of a professional psychologist. Before he even suspects Dimmesdale he is attracted to him not only because of

Dimmesdale's physical ailment but also because of his hypersensitive character, in which Chillingworth hopes to find the cause of the disease: "So Roger Chillingworth . . . strove to go deep into his patient's bosom, delving among his principles, prying into his recollections and probing everything with a cautious touch, like a treasure-seeker in a dark cavern" (p. 124). He notes the strange earnestness with which Dimmesdale defends Hester's right to her daughter at Bellingham's mansion. And as he notices Dimmesdale's symptoms of guilt, he becomes excited and digs even deeper. In chapter 10 because of an intuitive urge he bares the sleeping Dimmesdale's breast and revels in the joy and wonder of what he sees there. When Dimmesdale returns from the forest in chapter 20, Chillingworth perceives that there is a change in their relationship and that Dimmesdale now knows who he is. Near the end of the novel, his combined intelligence and intuition cause him to be suspicious and to seek out a certain ship's captain and discover Hester's plan of escape.

Like Chillingworth, Pearl is a creature of extraordinary awareness; but although she is intelligent, she is also innocent and amoral, and most of her perception of truth comes from intuition rather than conscious reasoning. As John Hart explains: "Cut off from the roots of the past, Pearl can judge action (precocious child that she is) not according to previous moral standards, but according to the amount of truth demonstrated to her. She acts always as her skeptical and innocent nature dictates." Because of her instinct for truth, she is acutely aware of her parents' guilt and shame. Therefore, she acts as a relentless agent of conscience, constantly reminding Hester and Arthur of their sin.

Even as a three-month-old baby Pearl perceives a relationship with Dimmesdale. When he speaks to Hester in the first scaffold scene, Pearl holds up her arms "with a half pleased, half plaintive murmur" (p. 67). As she grows older she becomes aware of the signs of her parents' guilt and constantly hints at a relationship between Hester and Arthur. In chapter 15 when Hester asks her if she knows why her mother wears the scarlet letter, she intuitively replies, "Truly do I! . . . It is for the same reason that the minister keeps his hand over his heart!" (pp. 178–79). Although she doesn't consciously recognize the relationship between her parents, and she certainly is incapable of making a moral judgment of them, she instinctively knows that there is a connection between them. Pearl is also aware of the changes in Dimmesdale during the holiday celebration at the end of the novel. She tells her mother that he acts differently toward her during the day than he does at night. She senses the minister's remoteness during the procession, but readily responds to his call after the sermon. She "flew to him, and clasped her arms about his knees" (p. 252), intuitively perceiving that he is about to do something significant.[10]

Therefore, both Chillingworth and Pearl have an intuitive awareness of guilt, shame, and truth. Part of Chillingworth's awareness, however, is cultivated. He can perceive truth by intuition and then use his power of reasoning to discover additional truths. He can also make moral judgments about what he perceives. However, Pearl can perceive truth only by intuition and instinct. She is incapable of effectively reasoning and making moral judgments about what she perceives.

In addition to their powers of intuition, Pearl and Chillingworth also share the trait of perversity. Chillingworth reveals his perverse nature in his interactions with Hester. In their prison interview he delights in torturing her by putting his finger on the scarlet letter to watch Hester squirm and by suggesting that she may have nightmares if she wears the letter to bed. He also smiles with pleasure to see Hester cringe at Bellingham's mansion when Pearl gives an unorthodox answer to Mr. Wilson's question. His perversity is also seen when he arranges to disrupt Hester's plan of escape at the end of the novel.

When Chillingworth employs his skill in psychology in a calculated plan to torment Dimmesdale, his perversity becomes diabolic. In order to gain revenge he devises a plan of excruciating mental torture for the minister, knowing exactly at which moments and in which ways to apply the screws. In chapter 10 he attacks Dimmesdale's belief that the sins and suffering of the body can be separated from those of the spirit. In this way he plants the seeds of doubt in the minister's mind and begins to destroy Dimmesdale's delusion that his soul has not been corrupted. After seven years of such persistent hammering at Dimmesdale's nervous temperament and sensitive conscience, Chillingworth achieves his fiendish purpose:

> The sufferer's conscience had been kept in an irritated state, the tendency of which was, not to cure by wholesome pain, but to disorganize and corrupt his spiritual being. Its result, on earth,

could hardly fail to be insanity, and hereafter, that eternal alienation from the Good and the True, of which madness is perhaps the
earthly type. [P. 193]

In the process of torturing Dimmesdale, Chillingworth has
transformed himself into the image of the devil. The villagers
consider him to be Satan's emissary, inhuman and diabolical.
When Hester sees his smile and scowl during the second scaffold scene, she thinks he looks like an archfiend, and the fiery
glare of his eyes reinforces her impression when she meets him
at the seashore: "In a word, old Roger Chillingworth was a
striking evidence of man's faculty of transforming himself into
a devil" (p. 170). Even little Pearl refers to him as the Black Man
when she sees him at the window in chapter 10. And Chillingworth himself knows that he has been transformed into a fiend
and tells Hester so in chapter 14:

"And what am I now?" demanded he, looking into her face, and
permitting the whole evil within him to be written on his features. "I
have already told thee what I am! A fiend!" [Pp. 172–73]

Like Chillingworth, Pearl also displays a perverse and malicious nature. In fact, according to Garlitz, "she has ten times the
perversity of ordinary children."[11] Using a naughty laugh to
punctuate her cruelty, she delights in hurting people, and claps
with joy when she causes Dimmesdale to shrink by tossing a
prickly burr at him. She also delights in chasing other children
and in pelting birds with pebbles and her mother's scarlet letter
with flowers. Her seeming lack of sympathy for human feeling
is also seen in the way she tortures both her mother and
Dimmesdale with her curiosity about their relationship and the
scarlet letter. Like Chillingworth, she intuitively knows the
right time and the right way to inflict the greatest amount of
punishment. "The torture inflicted by the intelligent touch of
Pearl's baby-hand" (p. 96) against the scarlet letter is felt by
Hester again and again throughout the novel. She shows
Hester the enormous "A" in the breastplate-mirror at Bellingham's mansion. She fashions an "A" from seaweed and
goads her mother unceasingly with questions about the letter
and Dimmesdale's hand-to-heart reflex in chapter 15. And to
compound the wound she has inflicted in the forest scene by
forcing Hester to replace the scarlet letter, Pearl immediately
kisses it. She similarly torments Dimmesdale during the second

scaffold scene by chiding him for treating her differently in daylight and by teasing him with her gibberish about Chillingworth. Likewise, in the forest scene she refuses to show him any affection and even washes off his undesired kiss.

Like Chillingworth's, Pearl's perversity also borders on the diabolic, and she is frequently referred to as a devil or an inhuman being. The townspeople call her a "demon off-spring" (p. 99). Chillingworth, the archfiend himself, notices Pearl's fiendish nature and asks Dimmesdale, "What, in Heaven's name, is she? Is the imp altogether evil?" (p. 134). Even Hester is aware of Pearl's seemingly evil nature:

> She fancied that she beheld, not her own miniature portrait, but another face in the small black mirror of Pearl's eye. It was a face, fiend-like, full of smiling malice, yet bearing the semblance of features that she had known full well, though seldom with a smile, and never with malice, in them. It was as if an evil spirit possessed the child, and had just then peeped forth in mockery. [P. 97]

Both Hester and Hawthorne agree that Pearl is basically inhuman, that she sometimes seems "incapable and unintelligent of human sorrow" (p. 93), and that she needs a deeply felt grief to humanize her.

Thus, Pearl and Chillingworth are both perverse, malicious, and somewhat inhuman. Both have fiendish smiles and a fiery glow—Chillingworth in his eyes and Pearl in her fanciful scarlet dress. Both have evil natures that cause Hester to shudder and the townspeople to label them demonic. And both take a sadistic delight in human torture and have a knack for effectively inducing that torture. However, Chillingworth's torture is cultivated and carefully planned, whereas Pearl's seems more instinctive and not consciously devised. In addition, their purposes for torment are different. In a sense, Chillingworth is cruel to be cruel, whereas Pearl is cruel to be kind. The purpose of Chillingworth's torture is destruction; the purpose of Pearl's torture is repentance.

Chillingworth's fiendishness has been aroused by intense jealousy. When he first sees Hester and Pearl on the scaffold, his reaction is significant:

> A writhing horror twisted itself across his features, like a snake gliding swiftly over them, and making one little pause, with all its wreathed intervolutions in open sight. His face darkened with some

> powerful emotion, which, nevertheless, he so instantaneously con-
> trolled by an effort of his will, that, save at a single moment, its
> expression might have passed for calmness. After a brief space, the
> convulsion grew almost imperceptible, and finally subsided into the
> depths of his nature. [P. 61]

Although he represses his instinctive emotional response, for
just a second his intense jealousy has been revealed. Deeply
wounded by Hester's sin and unable to obtain her love himself,
his only recourse is revenge against the man who did. His
previous calmness, kindness, and potential for good have been
perverted by a crime against his love; therefore, he will employ
all his skills toward avenging that crime. And the monomania
that eventually seizes him and causes him to inflict seven years
of excruciating torture upon his victim is sufficient proof of his
passion:

> Ever and anon, too, there came a glare of red light out of his eyes;
> as if the old man's soul were on fire, and kept on smouldering
> duskily within his breast, until, by some casual puff of passion, it was
> blown into momentary flame. This he repressed as speedily as
> possible, and strove to look as if nothing of the kind had happened.
> [P. 169]

Clearly then, Chillingworth's purpose is the destruction of Dimmesdale's spirit and the damnation of his soul.

Pearl's intuitive torture, however, has a quite different purpose, what Anne Marie McNamara refers to as "the angelic
purpose of redemption."[12] Pearl is not truly evil or demonic
because she is basically innocent and amoral, and her purpose is
to achieve the repentance of her parents. As Hyatt Waggoner
asserts, Pearl is morally neutral: "She is as incapable of deceit or
dishonesty as nature itself, and at times as unsympathetic. She is
not good or bad, because she is not responsible. . . . She is not
bad, she is merely natural."[13] Ironically, by innocently helping
to bring about the repentance of Dimmesdale, Pearl also gains
her own salvation. When Dimmesdale acknowledges that he is
Pearl's father at the end of the novel, he not only accomplishes
his own salvation but also saves Pearl from her natural, amoral
state. By confessing, the minister abandons the falsehood that
has been tormenting him, thereby achieving his own redemption. At the same time, he provides for Pearl an earthly father,
thereby humanizing her and rescuing her from an amoral state.

In this way he restores Pearl to both the human family and the moral order of the universe.

Obviously Pearl is not so evil and diabolical as Chillingworth. In fact, her inhuman, spiritlike quality and her mischievous, sometimes malicious elfishness make her more like a poltergeist than a devil. She has suffered a wrong through her parents' sin and is now functioning as the ghost or spirit of that sin. By haunting and tormenting her parents she hopes to gain redress for the wrong committed against her and to be released from her spirit form. In Pearl's case, however, the released spirit becomes human.

Few attempts have been made by the critics to explain the obvious similarities between Roger Chillingworth and Pearl. Hugh Maclean suggests that although they never exchange a word with each other, "Pearl is implicitly in his power by force of the mysterious drug"[14] which Chillingworth gives her in prison at the beginning of the novel. Maclean seems to be suggesting that Chillingworth is controlling Pearl throughout the novel, which might explain their similar behavior. Sandeen claims that by leaving his property to Pearl when he dies, Chillingworth "suggests his tacit admission that Dimmesdale in his last hour successfully usurped the role of father and husband."[15] This interpretation leads to the conclusion that, technically, since he is Hester's husband, Chillingworth is the only father that Pearl has until the end of the novel. Perhaps Hawthorne was trying to emphasize this subtle point by giving them similar character traits. When Pearl hears Dimmesdale's confession, she loses the inhuman traits of her surrogate father and gains the human ones of her natural father. Finally, Nina Baym suggests that Pearl and Chillingworth are similar because they perform an identical function. As Baym points out, both Pearl and Chillingworth are semi-human and mainly symbolic. Pearl stands in the same symbolic relationship to Hester as does Chillingworth to Dimmesdale. Thus, Pearl represents the sin that torments Hester; Chillingworth the sin that torments Dimmesdale.[16] Or perhaps the similarity between Pearl and Chillingworth is only accidental. Since Hawthorne uses them to perform the same function, as pricks of conscience, it is only natural that their characters have certain elements in common.

Whether Hawthorne was aware of the similarities of these two characters, and whether he made them alike for a particular reason, we can never know definitely, but the similarity still exists. Certainly the romance genre does not require fidelity of character and inherited character traits; but since Hawthorne frequently employs heredity, it is only natural to question his use of it in little Pearl. Why didn't he give her any of Dimmesdale's characteristics? Why is she so much like Chillingworth?

This analysis is not proposing a radical new interpretation of the novel—that Chillingworth is Pearl's natural father. Even though a fantastic creature like Pearl might take somewhat longer than the normal nine months to develop, the details of the novel clearly indicate that Hester and Chillingworth have been separated for two years. Nevertheless, it is noteworthy that Chillingworth and Pearl are oddly, almost supernaturally, similar. Indeed it seems strange that the townspeople, in their avid desire to discover Pearl's father, never suspect Chillingworth. It is clear, though, why they overlook Arthur Dimmesdale and even refuse to believe him when he finally does confess.

Notes

1. Ernest Sandeen, *"The Scarlet Letter* as a Love Story," *PMLA* 77 (1962): 433.

2. Nathaniel Hawthorne, *The Scarlet Letter,* vol. 2 in the Centenary edition (Columbus: Ohio State University Press, 1962), p. 116; all page numbers cited in parentheses in the text are from this edition of *The Scarlet Letter.*

3. Seymour Katz, "'Character,' 'Nature,' and Allegory in *The Scarlet Letter,"* *Nineteenth-Century Fiction* 23 (1968): 5.

4. Terence Martin, *Nathaniel Hawthorne,* rev. ed. (Boston: Twayne, 1983), p. 111.

5. Ibid., p. 120.

6. Barbara Garlitz, "Pearl: 1850–1955," *PMLA* 72 (1957): 697. It was believed that children inherited moral tendencies from their parents, and that parents would transmit the moral faculties which were predominating in them at the time of the child's conception. A mother's state of mind and feelings during pregnancy could affect the temper of her child. Therefore, Garlitz claims that Pearl has inherited sin and moral disease from her parents (pp. 697–98). Garlitz's theory is a sound one for explaining Pearl's defiance in terms of Hester's mental agony, but its "inherited moral disease" aspect is questionable if Hester believes that she hasn't really committed an immoral act or if Pearl is considered an amoral creature.

7. Several critics have been particularly harsh with Dimmesdale—much more harsh than I would care to be—finding in him no redeeming qualities whatsoever. Terence Martin, for example, emphasizes Dimmesdale's excessive pride and egotism, which lead to his hypocrisy. According to Martin, Dimmesdale is unwilling to sacrifice his self-admiration and his splendid public image:

With all his physical and psychological debility, which makes him seem weak and gives him the posture of a moral invalid deserving of pity (or perhaps contempt), Dimmesdale is afflicted with a devious pride. He cannot surrender an identity which brings him the adulation of his parishioners, the respect and praise of his peers. His contortions in the guise of humility only add to the public admiration which, in turn, feeds an ego fundamentally intent on itself. [*Nathaniel Hawthorne,* p. 113]

William H. Nolte, in "Hawthorne's Dimmesdale: A Small Man Gone Wrong," *New England Quarterly* 38 (1965), goes a step further by emphasizing Dimmesdale's narcissism. Nolte claims that nothing matters to Dimmesdale but himself, that "his 'love' for Hester was no more than a flirtation with the devil (in his eyes); and his love for God, or the strictures of his peculiar God, was a debasing form of self-aggrandizement, darkly tinged with self-abuse" (p. 172). Nolte further claims that Dimmesdale's hollowness and self-pity are nowhere more obvious than in his weak and unheroic confession at the end of the novel. He thinks that he can make amends for seven years of cowardice and hypocrisy and gain a chance to be saved by confessing his sin before he dies. "It appears to me evident that Arthur's confession cost him absolutely nothing, that indeed it was an act designed to win him immortal life" (p. 185).

8. Darrel Abel, "Hawthorne's Pearl: Symbol and Character," *Journal of English Literary History* 18 (1951): 53.

9. John E. Hart, *"The Scarlet Letter—*One Hundred Years After," *New England Quarterly* 23 (1950): 386.

10. Gloria C. Erlich, in *Family Themes and Hawthorne's Fiction* (New Brunswick, N.J.: Rutgers University Press, 1984), attributes Pearl's intuitive ability to the intensity of her search for a father: "Lacking overt clues, she developed uncanny intuitive gifts" and became "a bundle of searching intuition" (p. 29).

11. Garlitz, "Pearl," p. 691.

12. Anne Marie McNamara, "The Character of Flame: The Function of Pearl in *The Scarlet Letter,"* *American Literature* 27 (1956): 553.

13. Hyatt H. Waggoner, *Hawthorne: A Critical Study,* rev. ed. (Cambridge: Harvard University Press, 1963), p. 152.

14. Hugh N. Maclean, "Hawthorne's *Scarlet Letter:* 'The Dark Problem of This life,'" *American Literature* 27 (1955): 18.

15. Sandeen, *"Scarlet Letter,"* p. 433.

16. Nina Baym, "Passion and Authority in *The Scarlet Letter,"* *New England Quarterly* 43 (1970): 217.

Thoreau's Philosophy of Rhetorical Invention

Richard H. Dillman

St. Cloud State University

IN addition to his importance as a stylist, a naturalist, and an apostle of self-reliance, Henry David Thoreau was also a philosopher of rhetoric. He wrote extensively on rhetorical issues in his journals, and he commented occasionally on this subject in his correspondence. Thoreau revised his work consistently, often developing ideas from journal entry to lecture and then into prose. He thought substantially about the problems of composing, paying close attention to ways that writers could invent or discover material, to problems of adapting discourse to the needs and prejudices of an audience, and to issues of style and form. In his journals and partly in his correspondence, Thoreau developed a coherent philosophy of rhetoric containing perceptive ideas on the art of effective discourse. He addressed invention, style, and arrangement or form—the three traditional canons of rhetorical study that apply to both speaking and writing—in his comments on rhetoric, devoting considerable attention to each area. I propose in this essay to describe and explain Thoreau's thoughts on rhetorical invention, demonstrating in the process that he was a thoughtful student of this important area of rhetoric. A full explication of Thoreau's thoughts on rhetoric would require a book-length manuscript; hence, I intend this study to be an initial step toward this fuller explanation. Moreover, this essay may help us see Thoreau as an important figure in the history of American rhetoric.[1]

Much of Thoreau's commentary on rhetoric was concerned with the art of inventing or discovering ideas and subject matter to use in discourse. As an area of study, invention involves examining methods of generating details and arguments and studying methods of inquiry. A philosophy of rhetorical invention legitimately asks this question, How does a writer or speaker probe his or her subject in order to better understand it? At the time that Thoreau was writing about invention in his journals, rhetorical theory in the United States was changing significantly. The influence of classical rhetoric was waning and being replaced by a theory based largely on the psychological rhetoric of George Campbell and Richard Whately. At Harvard where Thoreau studied rhetoric from 1833 to 1837, Edward Tyrell Channing, the Boylston Professor of Rhetoric and Oratory, relied extensively on psychological rhetoric and even used Campbell's and Whately's texts in his courses.[2] Essentially, the approach to rhetoric used by Channing and by Campbell and Whately can be called managerial; that is, it was a rhetorical theory that ignored invention and addressed instead the problems of effectively communicating material that was already known. Douglas Ehninger explains that in the early nineteenth century there was a "growing romantic distrust of the status and topics of invention as artificial aides to invention that was supported by the growing recognition that the scientific method provided an investigatory procedure adaptable to many disciplines."[3]

Rhetoric was thus seen as having almost no responsibility for what might be said on a subject. To George Campbell, in his *Philosophy of Rhetoric,* the task of supplying subject matter for discourse was assigned to the field of logic or to the appropriate substantive subject.[4] Channing, Thoreau's rhetoric professor, held essentially the same view of invention, explaining in his *Lectures* that wide reading provides student writers with "facts, thoughts, and illustrations for their writing."[5] Channing thus saw books as the major source of ideas for the writer's task.[6] There was no substitute in Channing's approach for a well-stocked mind. As a result, there was essentially no theory of invention in the Harvard rhetoric curriculum of Thoreau's time. Invention was ignored or glossed over while the topics of style, form, and correctness were emphasized. Thoreau, without benefit of academic rhetorical theory, developed his own philosophy of rhetorical invention that was clearly in harmony with the philosophy of American Transcendentalism. Most of Thoreau's comments on invention appear in his journal between the years of 1850 and 1852 when he was deeply involved in expanding and shaping *Walden* and working on its third and fourth versions.[7] Thoreau wrote *Walden* over a period of nearly six years from 1848 until March 1854, when he finally delivered his manuscript to Ticknor and Fields of Boston. He revised it seven times, tested some chapters on the lecture platform, and developed several journal entries into sections of *Walden*.[8] However, his journal comments on invention that do appear both before the composition of *Walden* and after its publication are remarkably consistent with commentary that he made while he was composing *Walden*.

I will now describe and explain Thoreau's philosophy of invention. While we cannot credit him with giving rhetorical theory a new direction because most of his thoughts on rhetoric were neither public nor published during the nineteenth century, we can easily see links between his philosophy of invention and approaches to rhetoric widely used in late twentieth-century American schools and colleges. In the interest of clarity, I will divide my discussion into the following sections: an explanation of Thoreau's thoughts on finding writing topics, his thoughts on the art of discovery, and his extensive commentary on the use of the writer's journal as a source of ideas. To explain his philosophy of invention, however, I must first explain the psychological and physical conditions that Thoreau felt contributed to effective discovery. He felt quite strongly that the arts of invention must be accompanied by the right blend of physical and psychological conditions. Writers don't work in vacuums, and one's degree of physical activity and one's psychological state surely influence composing behavior. Discovery, Thoreau felt, must be timely, for the writer's time as a writer was short, fleeting, and unpredictable, and he, accordingly, advised writers in 1852 to "write as if thy time were short. . . . Drain the cup of inspiration to its last dregs," and take advantage of all inspiration.[9] Writers must clearly write when they feel the "heat" to write, a point that he illustrated with the following homely image: "When the farmer burns a hole in his yoke, he carries the hot iron quickly from the fire to the wood, for every moment it is less effectual to penetrate (pierce) it. It must be used instantly, or it is useless. The writer who postpones the recording of his thoughts uses an iron which has cooled to burn a hole with" (*J* 3:293, in 1852). In Thoreau's view, the time at which we write affects the energy that we can bring to our work. Moreover, on this same subject in 1851, he advises us not to fear writing on the spur of the moment or writing spontaneously when he addresses the common idea that good writing should be well planned. We can always reconsider our remarks later by "reforming" them (*J* 3:231–32, in 1852). In 1857, in a clearer statement on revision, he advises writers to sometimes make two versions of any occurrence or description—first, to make an initial report when inspired and to later, in a second report, add additional details that come to mind (*J* 9:300). This philosophy of revision, while clearly concerned with invention, can also help writers attempt spontaneous writing, since initial drafts could always be revised.

Thoreau also saw a definite connection between physical movement and writing. For example, in 1851, he explains that "the moment my legs begin to move my thoughts begin to flow," and "only while we are in action is the circulation perfect" (*J* 2:404–5). Referring here to both blood and mental circulation, he suggests that physical activity can help loosen us up for writing and thus aid discovery. He would argue, I think, that exercise can help clarify our thinking. "The writing which consists with habitual sitting is mechanical, wooden, dull to read" (*J* 2:405, in 1851). Now let me turn to the main elements of Thoreau's philosophy of invention.

The Writer's Subject

How do writer's find their subjects? Thoreau devoted considerable attention to answering this question in his journals. He felt that subjects and themes for writing must come from experience and a deeply lived life, and he maintains that effective writers must completely assimilate their subjects. We should not, he tells us, write about things that we are merely acquainted with but write instead about those things that we intimately know (*J* 11:446, in 1859). The true writer, he advises, should avoid pandering to the popular taste in choosing topics and thus avoid compromising his personal integrity by choosing topics to please popular opinion. "He should write in the stream that interests him the most," he claims in 1851, and he should try to "clear a new field instead of manuring the old" (*J* 3:144, 156). Certainly originality is important in choosing subjects, but that by itself is not enough to insure reader interest. "A great writer," he tells us in 1861, "can make the history of his parish more interesting than another's history of the world" (*J* 14:330).

To find the right subject, writers must also probe several

topics and try several points of view. It is wise to write on many subjects and themes, he asserts in 1851, to find the true and inspiring one. Moreover, he goes on to tell us on the same page that "it is not in vain that the mind turns aside this way or that; follow its leading, apply it whither it inclines to go; probe the universe in a myriad of points." In a characteristic hyperbole in the same passage, he claims that "you must try a thousand themes before you find the right one" (*J* 2:457). Ideas must be tried and dropped if found wanting. Clearly Thoreau is open-minded in his discussion of methods of choosing subjects and themes, emphasizing that there are "innumerable avenues to a perception of the truth" (*J* 2:457).

Personal integrity, a main theme throughout Thoreau's work, is also important to the writer. He explains in 1851 that writers and speakers should speak for themselves and not for others (*J* 3:157). Keeping our authentic personalities behind our writing should help tell us who the writer is, where he has been, and "what he has thought" (*J* 3:99, in 1851). Thus, he calls for an authentic personal voice that is reflected in the choice of subject matter and theme. This voice, moreover, must come from "a genuine and contented life," one that "must have the essence or oil of himself, tried out of the fat of his experience and joy" (*J* 9:195, in 1856). The lack of freedom of speech that Thoreau felt was typical of his time he also saw as connected to the problem of choosing appropriate subjects for writing and for speaking. He argues that "the voice that arises from public forums is not so brave and so cheering as that which rises from the frog ponds of the land" (*J* 11:325, in 1858). The frogs, if I read this correctly, have more authentic voices than the preachers and other public speakers of his time. In Thoreau's view, then, choosing a subject to please an audience instead of oneself could only weaken the writer's voice and diminish personal integrity. A strong personal voice requires that writers choose subjects with which they are comfortable and think are important. Let me now turn to Thoreau's thoughts on discovering material for writing after the subject has been chosen.

The Art of Discovery

Thoreau spent considerable time exploring the art of discovery in his journals. He was concerned with the processes by which thinkers, speakers, and writers discover meaning and with modes of interpreting experience. In fact, he repeatedly refers to the writer as a seer and examiner, arguing that the ability to see and experience the world deeply is a major source of the writer's power. He tells us in 1859 that commonplace thoughts that "run in ruts" or "automatic" thoughts were based on semi-conscious sensuous impressions that writers must try to avoid (*J* 12:156). "A man must see, before he can say," he prophetically states, and by "say" he meant considerably more than reporting experience scientifically. He believed instead that objective observation is only myth: in Thoreau's view, there is no such thing. He claims in 1854, the year in which *Walden* was published, that to be truly interesting a writer's observations must be subjective (*J* 6:236–37). "A fact truely and absolutely stated" acquires a mythological and universal significance when it is removed from the realm of common sense he also tells us earlier in his third journal (p. 85, in 1851). To the open mind, he argues, small facts suggest large ideas. He clearly stands against the method of scientific reporting then growing in popularity as a method of investigation adaptable to many areas of learning. He explains further that the eyes of science are barren and that scientific perception does not lead quickly to higher meaning. To see scientifically in the Lockean sense, he believed, is to see superficially and to understand facts as they are related to institutions like the military, the universities, and the government (*J* 3:85–86, in 1851).

Thoreau had little sympathy for Lockean empirical perception, and an early letter written to his sister Helen in 1838 soon after his graduation from Harvard provides a glimpse of his unhappiness with the mental philosophy taught at Harvard. He explains that the mental philosophers "have squeezed the infinite mind into a compass that would nonplus a surveyor of eastern lands—making imagination and memory to lie still in their respective apartments like ink-stands and wafers in a lady's escritoire."[10] Thoreau saw the perceiving, discovering mind as larger, more complex, than Locke's tabula rasa theory of perception could envision, and he clearly understood the empirical philosophy of Locke and the associationist philosophy of Dugald Stewart, the two mental philosophies studied at Harvard during his student days, as limiting a thinker's or writer's discovery and vision. Thoreau understood perception here in transcendentalist terms, emphasizing its subjectivity and the role of the self in the act of perceiving. His rejection of the Lockean empirical approach to discovery surely reflects the romantic bias of his time. To Thoreau, however, using the subjective mode of observation wasn't enough.

To this he added having the right attitude toward discovery. For the discovery process to work well, the effective writer should also observe selectively. Thoreau recognizes the essential selectivity of perception when he points out in 1857 that we discover "only the world we look for" (J 9:466) and that we don't see many things precisely because we aren't looking for them. We discover new ideas, he tells us, if we only look hard enough and selectively enough. Freshness of perceptions is also important to discovery, but he explains that this freshness must be tempered by distance (J 4:20, in 1852). In his journal of 1857, he explains that the most poetic and truest account of objects is generally by those who first observe them (J 9:232). Later, however, a day or two distance from the writer's experience will help temper the freshness, thus helping him evaluate his previous jottings (J 4:20).

The writer should also be able to see experience in concrete terms. He tells us that "a writer who does not speak from concrete experience often uses torpid words, wooden or lifeless words, such words as 'humanitary' which have a paralysis in their tails" (J 4:225, in 1852). He also describes the writings of academics as lifeless, overly abstract, and lacking the power of observed experience because it is too far removed from the concrete world. "The life of learned professors has been almost as inhuman and wooden as a rain gauge," he declares (J 6:238, in 1854).

The power of memory and the use of analogies are also important components of Thoreau's philosophy of invention. Good writers, he suggests, should draw on their long-term memories. Years after an experience, Thoreau tells us that his memory provided him with useful information when "only the most significant facts" appeared to him (J 9:311). The writer should also use analogies for discovery as often as possible, employing them to connect otherwise disparate areas of experience in distinct ways. This concept of analogy, moreover, reflects his strong ties to nature, especially when he claims that "all perception of truth is the detection of an analogy; we reason from our hands to our head" (J 2:462–63, in 1851). Through the concrete—those things experienced here with the hands—we would be able to experience the abstract. Later, in 1860, he explains that in language use "we admire any closeness to the physical fact which in all language is the symbol of the spiritual" (*J* 13:145). Implicit in his transcendental theory of language is the notion that writers should strive to use concrete language and avoid an abstract style when possible.

Thoreau's philosophy for discovering ideas may accurately be called organic because he emphasizes the generating power of the writer's thoughts. He saw the acts of writing and thinking as processes in themselves. We generate ideas as we write because one idea leads to another; ideas lead to further ideas. He tells us in 1860, near the end of his writing life, that "the Scripture rule 'unto him that hath shall be given' is true of composition. The more you have thought and written on a given theme, the more you can still write. Thought breeds thought. It grows under your hands" (*J* 13:145). This very contemporary notion of writing suggests that planning isn't always necessary; writing, in essence, activates the brain, and thoughts suggest other thoughts in ways that we can't always identify but that nevertheless work. Because it has the quality of unfolding or growing as a tree or plant grows, branch giving way to branch, bud giving way to leaf, this process has an organic quality.

The Writer's Journal

Thoreau places great emphasis on the writer's journal as both an avenue for discovery and as a place to test his thoughts. He wrote in his fourteen-volume journal from 1837 through 1861, later revising and polishing his journal materials into publishable form. Much of *Walden,* for example, and many of his reform essays and nature pieces first began as journal entries. James Lyndon Shanley, in his *The Making of Walden,* has ably examined the genesis of *Walden* from journal to published text and has traced Thoreau's editing and revision processes. Because Thoreau's journal was the source of numerous ideas that later evolved into *Walden* and other pieces, his comments on the journal as a discovery device are especially instructive.

He was very conscious of the role that journals played in his life as a writer, and he developed a comprehensive philosophy for their use. Basically, Thoreau thought of the journal as a seedbed for ideas—as a place to plant ideas that he would later develop (*J* 2:101, in 1850). In his third journal, written when he was revising *Walden* in 1852, he explained how and why journals should be used. Because he was busy composing, revising, and shaping *Walden* from his journal materials and from his memories, he must have been extremely conscious of his journal's role in the growth of his manuscript. First, he saw it as a place to record choice experiences that would later inspire him. Thus the journal would help him remember his best hours and stimulate his thoughts when he was far from the original experiences. The journal, he tells us, can rescue our thoughts and feelings from oblivion and help writers renew their associations with their loftiest ideas. He explained further that each recorded thought "is a nest-egg by the side of which more will be laid," and these same thoughts can later become a frame for the development of additional ideas (*J* 3:217, in 1852). Thus ideas written in a journal will contribute to generating additional ideas, and Thoreau again emphasizes an organic approach to invention.

Thoreau also stresses the suggestive power of the journal. When he returned to read his entries, he often felt that the act of reading disconnected thoughts and bringing them into juxtaposition would suggest a "new field in which to labor" or a new topic or theme on which to write. The journal is a place full of fragments that will later allow the writer to make wholes from parts; it will, he explains, "suggest the harmonious completion" of unfinished pictures (*J* 3:217). The journal, too, was a relatively serious affair for Thoreau, who saw no room for jesting in this type of writing (*J* 3:222).

In 1856, two years after the publication of *Walden,* he also defined the journal as a record of experiences and growth, not a preserve of things well done or said, and he explains further that "the charm of the journal must consist of a certain greenness, though freshness, and not in maturity" (*J* 8:134). It is not a place for fully developed, edited ideas. Writing in the journal is also process-centered, and it becomes a repository of ideas that authors might otherwise forget or waste (*J* 1:206, in 1841; 2:143, in 1851).

Thoreau also understood the journal as a vehicle for expressing the self. Writers should record experiences as they affect themselves describing, for example, the weather or the nature of the day as they affect a writer's feelings (*J* 7:171, in 1855). He also felt that joy was the main feeling to be expressed in the journal; it was a place for optimistic thoughts, a book, he claims, that shall contain "a record of all your joy, your ecstasy" (*J*

4:223, in 1852), a notion that reflects Thoreau's own romantic idealism. He explained, too, how journals should be written by suggesting specific techniques that writers might use. First, the writer should compose the journal for him or herself as the main reader since journals aren't meant for other audiences. Except for himself as his own reader, Thoreau claimed that his thoughts sail off to the gods.[11] Writers must also endeavor to make their journal writing more concentrated and concise than public writing, omitting all flourishes and stylistic ornamentation from its pages (*J* 1:312, in 1842).

Distance from the writer's subject matter is also important to his philosophy of journal writing, and he encourages writers to return to the journals to add additional material. Making two entries on the same topic helped Thoreau's thinking. He explained that he would make an original record of an incident and later add a second reaction to that incident. In the second entry, he records the omissions that will often be "the most significant and poetic part of the journal," claiming, in a poetic tone, that "men and things of today are wont to lie fairer and truer in tomorrow's memory" (*J* 9:306, in 1857).

He also felt that journal writings should be unplanned. Writers should not choose their subjects strategically and should not plan their entries. He wrote what moved him or concerned him on a given day, and he recorded thoughts that he felt were "allied to life" (*J* 3:239, in 1852). Most importantly, I think, he speaks of his journal as a route to discovery where a writer might, metaphorically at least, "discover the wealth of India" (*J* 1:182, in 1841).

Besides the discovery function, Thoreau also identified an important therapeutic use for journals. In an early college essay written in 1837 on the assigned topic of journals in writing, he explained how they might help people sort out their lives:

> But if each one would employ a certain portion of each day looking back upon the time which has passed, and in writing down his thoughts and feelings, in reckoning up his daily gains that he may be able to detect whatever false coins have crept into his coffers, and, as it were, in settling accounts with his mind, not only would his daily experiences be greatly increased, since his feelings and ideas would be more clearly defined, but he would be ready to turn over a new leaf, having carefully perused the preceding one, and would not continue to glance carelessly over the same page without being able to distinguish a new one.[12]

Although this passage is not written in Thoreau's mature style or during his mature years, it does identify another dimension to his thinking about journal writing. It can be used to gain perspective on a day's events and to sort out the complexities of experience. Although he doesn't discuss how the journal might help to provide emotional release or catharsis, I think that his comments point in that direction. Today thousands use journals therapeutically, and they are frequently used by counselors and psychologists to help their patients gain perspective on their lives. Thoreau anticipated this late twentieth-century use for journals.

Thoreau saw the self as the main engine of creativity and inventiveness. The open, thinking self in contact with the world generates the topics and material for the writer's work. This self, moreover, is encouraged to modify external reality—that is, to be subjective and ignore the Lockean mode of perception. Within the individual lie powerful resources for invention that do not need assistance from the classical topics of invention or heuristics or such planning devices as outlining. This concept of invention clearly reflects the American transcendentalist notion of the self as an inner consciousness that needs only to break through successive layers of social conditioning to express truth and release its creative energies. It is also a self that is unconcerned with the needs of audience or the claims of readers. The rhetorician is encouraged to say what he thinks or feels without the need to conform to his readers' expectations and values. Moreover, this philosophy encourages writers to maintain an honest speaking voice and thereby retain personal integrity.

Thoreau consistently emphasizes the process nature of invention by stressing the process of probing and testing subject matter, the process of writing as a mode of discovery, and the process of using journals as a source of ideas. In this sense, his philosophy of invention has the organic quality mentioned earlier since he saw writing as growing, developing, and moving through stages. This notion of invention looks toward a theory of revision, especially since much of what he says about generating ideas can be applied recursively to various stages of the writing process. For example, in the final revising stages of composition, a writer could surely refer back to his or her journal or attempt additional, unplanned writing on pertinent topics. This organic approach in which ideas lead to other ideas is philosophically optimistic as is Thoreau's belief in the rich creative abilities of the inner self. In essence, believing in the efficacy of this approach to invention requires a certain leap of faith and a belief in the metaphysical, such as Thoreau and Emerson certainly had. If we believe, as Thoreau apparently did, that the creative self is linked to and is part of a universal spirit loosely called the oversoul that somehow unifies the world, then Thoreau's philosophy of invention requires that the composing self be partly, at least, in tune with this underlying spirit.

The notion of organic invention also reflects Thoreau's conception of the growth process in the natural world. Ideas lead to other ideas like seeds lead to plants or buds to leaves. This process is somewhat like the thawing of the hillside in the "Spring" chapter of *Walden,* where Thoreau describes the thawing hillside as resembling the form of a leaf—as "sand foliage," with veins branching off in several directions and later subdividing. Here he states prophetically that "it seemed that this one hillside illustrated the principle of all the operations of nature. The Maker of this earth but patented a leaf."[13] In like manner, the writer's ideas grow larger and more complex. On the same page of *Walden,* he also tells us that "there is nothing inorganic," a statement that seems to apply as well to the process of invention as it does to the natural world. Here, too, we see a concept of growth typical of American transcendentalist thinking.

Finally, I think we must understand Thoreau's philosophy of invention as being concerned with epistemology, and thus as being closely connected to the ways that individuals see the world. As you see, so you will say, he tells us. The emphasis on seeing is crucial here because the ability to see clearly and perceptively is a key to generating material for writing. The skillful writer must develop keen powers of observation unencumbered by the blinders of conformity. Seeing clearly and perceptively leads to understanding, which in turn may lead to effective writing.

If the writer's mode of seeing influences the writer's mode of saying, then we have the seeds of an epistemological approach to style too. If on successive days, we observe, say, the same stream or field and see them differently, depending on our mood, we may also express our thoughts in different ways. In this framework, invention and style then become inseparable. Thus invention leads to style, and style grows out of an epistemological approach to invention. Thought then clearly leads to form.

This important idea clearly separates Thoreau's notion of invention from the classical concept of discovery that had fallen from grace before Thoreau entered Harvard. The epistemological approach to invention and style clearly stands against the Ciceronian approach to style taught at Harvard until about 1819,[14] which held essentially that ideas can be stated in a variety of different forms without changing their meaning. That is, ideas can be decorated or ornamented to suit different audiences or purposes. Finally, under Thoreau's philosophy, a change in style would also create a change in meaning.

Notes

1. Some theories of rhetoric popular in nineteenth-century America include the psychological rhetoric of George Campbell and Richard Whately, the belletristic (neoclassical) rhetoric of Hugh Blair, and the tradition of classical rhetoric whose influence was declining in the early years of the century. For an excellent discussion of nineteenth-century American rhetoric see Albert Kitzhaber, "Rhetoric in American Colleges, 1850–1900" (Ph. D. diss., University of Washington, 1953).

2. Dorothy Anderson, "Channing's Definition of Rhetoric," *Speech Monographs* 14 (1947): 81–86.

3. Douglas Ehninger, ed., *The Elements of Rhetoric* by Richard Whately (Carbondale: Southern Illinois University Press, 1969), p. xxvii.

4. Ibid.

5. Edward T. Channing, *Lectures Read to the Seniors in Harvard College,* ed. Dorothy Anderson and Waldo Braden (Carbondale: Southern Illinois University Press, 1968), pp. 191–92.

6. Ibid., pp. 192–93.

7. For further discussion of Thoreau's Harvard education in rhetoric see Richard H. Dillman, "Thoreau's Harvard Education in Rhetoric and Composition: 1833–1837," *Thoreau Journal Quarterly* 13, nos. 3–4 (1981): 47–62.

8. Walter Harding, *The Days of Henry Thoreau: A Biography* (New York: Dover, 1982), pp. 330–32.

9. Henry David Thoreau, *The Journal of Henry David Thoreau,* ed. Bradford Torrey and Francis H. Allen, 14 vols. (New York: Dover, 1962), 3:221; hereafter *J,* with volume and page numbers cited in the text.

10. Henry David Thoreau, *The Correspondence of Henry David Thoreau,* ed. Carl Bode and Walter Harding (New York: New York University Press, 1958), p. 29.

11. Thoreau's idea that his thoughts sail off to the gods appears in Henry David Thoreau, *Journal: Volume 1: 1837–1844,* ed. John C. Broderick, Center for the Editions

of American Authors edition (Princeton, N.J.: Princeton University Press, 1981), p. 220. This idea does not appear in Torrey and Allen's 1962 edition of the journals, cited in n. 9, above.

12. Henry David Thoreau, *Early Essays and Miscellanies* (Princeton, N.J.: Princeton University Press, 1975), pp. 8–9.

13. Henry David Thoreau, *The Illustrated Walden*, ed. J. Lyndon Shanley, Center for the Editions of American Authors edition (Princeton, N.J.: Princeton University Press, 1973), p. 308.

14. See Anderson and Braden's introduction to Channing, *Lectures*, pp. ix–xx, for a succinct account of the rhetoric program at Harvard in the early nineteenth century. For an account of the changes in the Boylston Professorship at Harvard see Ronald Reid, "The Boylston Professorship of Rhetoric and Oratory—1806–1904," *Quarterly Journal of Speech* 45 (1959): 239–57.

Thoreau's Philosophy of Audience

Richard H. Dillman

St. Cloud State University

IN his journals and partly in his correspondence, Henry David Thoreau developed a comprehensive philosophy of rhetoric. He frequently discussed such aspects of rhetoric as invention, form, style, sentence structure, effective word choice, and the writer's or speaker's relationship with his or her audience, and he was concerned with the tension between the rhetorician's need to speak with personal integrity and the sometimes compelling need to adapt discourse to the concerns and expectations of the audience. He saw this tension, moreover, as crucial to the act of writing and to speaking before an audience.[1]

Thoreau developed a philosophy of audience that was strongly tied to American transcendentalist notions of the self and that reflected key elements of romantic thought. In this essay, I will explain and interpret Thoreau's thoughts on the rhetorical problem of audience adaptation and also illustrate the dynamic evolution of these thoughts as they developed throughout his career as lecturer and author. This essay, furthermore, will also present a case study of his internal struggle with the tensions between personal self-expression and the demands of his readers and listeners. By a philosophy of audience, I mean a coherent body of thought about such audience-related topics as ingratiation with readers or listeners, adapting discourse to an audience, the writer's or speaker's stance toward audience, and methods of analyzing audiences. This examination of Thoreau's philosophy of audience will also help modern scholars understand part of Thoreau's thinking about rhetoric.

His thoughts on audience are particularly interesting since he faced audience problems from the positions of lecturer, essayist, and writer of nonfiction prose. He moved between the world of formal oral discourse and that of the prose stylist. In fact, many of his essays and indeed chapters of *Walden* began as lectures delivered to New England audiences. He often revised his lectures into essays, and hence his listeners' reactions must have played a role in his revisions into prose. He was writing and speaking in a transitional rhetorical world in which he moved often rapidly between oral and written discourse. In early nineteenth-century America oral modes of discourse were often in fact the models for such forms as the written polemic and the persuasive essay for which Thoreau was well known. Formal oral discourse and written prose forms were more closely connected in American culture than they are today.[2]

Thoreau often struggled with the dilemma of being true to his own voice and the need to be understood by his audiences. His lectures, which he began delivering during his first year out of college in 1838 and continued until shortly before his death in 1862, were usually read from prepared, written scripts. He often referred to writing his lectures, and many of them were in fact early drafts for his published essays and books. From 1848 to about 1853, Thoreau tried out drafts of sections of *Walden* such as "Economy" and "Where I Lived and What I Lived For" on audiences around Concord. Later, he would take these audience reactions into account when he revised his drafts.

Thoreau began lecturing seriously for income about 1848, when he also lived at Walden Pond, because he needed to supplement his small earnings from surveying and writing. According to Walter Harding, Thoreau's modern biographer, and Frank Sanborn, Thoreau's contemporary, his lectures were composed by expanding his journal entries; he later would often expand these lectures into essays.[3] In fact, Thoreau described this technique in the following way in his journal: "From all the points of the compass, from the earth beneath and the heavens above, have come these inspirations, and been duly entered in the order of their arrival in the [Thoreau's] journal. Thereafter, when the time arrived, they were winnowed into lectures, and again, in due time, from lectures into essays."[4] Harding tells us that Thoreau was persuaded to write *Walden* by his townsmen's favorable reactions to his Walden lectures, which he first delivered in 1847.

Most of his journal entries on the audience topic appeared

between 1855 and about 1860 when he completed most of his life's difficult writing and lecturing challenges. In 1854, he had finished the last of his seven revisions of *Walden* and finally published his major work. Moreover, *A Week on the Concord and Merrimack Rivers*, published in 1849, had failed to find an audience, and Thoreau was left owning most of the original edition. He had also delivered "On the Duty of Civil Disobedience" as a lecture in 1849, publishing it in the same year, and in 1853 the editors of *Putnam's Monthly* rejected publishing a part of *A Yankee in Canada* because that book's "heresies" would offend readers.[5] In 1858, toward the end of this period, James Russell Lowell, in Thoreau's viewpoint, too freely edited an important sentence from his essay on the Maine Woods that Lowell had published in the *Atlantic Monthly*. Apparently Lowell felt that the sentence "It [a pine tree] is as immortal as I am and perchance will go to as high a heaven, there to tower over me still" was too pantheistic for his readers.[6] Clearly irritated by this action, Thoreau explained to Lowell in a letter that "The editor has, in this case, no more right to omit a sentiment, than to insert one, or put words in my mouth."[7]

By the period from 1855 to 1860, then, Thoreau had confronted the problems of audience adaptation, and by 1860, he had formulated his thoughts on audience. He had experienced editorial censorship; he had considered his audiences' reactions to many of his lectures; and he had learned that readers were not attracted by *A Week on the Concord and Merrimack Rivers*. His well-earned philosophy of audience was derived from the dynamics of real interaction between speaker, writer, and audience and, accordingly, was far removed from textbook abstractions on the subject. Thoreau also had his greatest success as lecturer during his period of extensive commentary on audience. Two impassioned lectures that he later revised into essays—"A Plea for Captain John Brown" (1859) and "The Last Days of Captain John Brown" (1860)—were both energetically presented and effective with their audiences. These essays, in which Thoreau spoke from a sense of urgency and high moral commitment, grew out of his experience with Concord's strong abolitionist movement, the Harper's Ferry incident, and the government's subsequent treatment of John Brown. Nevertheless, Thoreau was not always this successful as a lecturer.

He generally was an ineffective lecturer, largely because he was not an effective speaker. He had an unfortunate minor speech defect manifested in an odd pronunciation of the letter *r* that Thoreau's friend Channing claimed had a "sort of burr in it,"[8] and he did not have an inspiring presence as a speaker or a very flexible voice. He also failed to make eye contact with his audience, choosing instead to keep his eyes fixed to his notes. Harding tells us that he was only able to truly excite his listeners when he was involved with the fight for justice as he was with the John Brown lectures. His humor sometimes helped his travel lectures to succeed, but his transcendental essays often failed because his subtle, intellectual humor was too often lost on his listeners.[9] Certainly Thoreau's weak lecturing skills must have influenced his thoughts and feelings about audience.

Let me now examine Thoreau's philosophy of audience as he developed it in his journals, his correspondence, and in the "Reading" chapter of *Walden*. Although most of his commentary on audience lies in his journals, he also devoted some attention to activities of readers in the "Reading" section of *Walden*.

Because Thoreau was committed to expressing his version of the truth, he often found himself unsympathetic to his audience's values and interests. Moreover, the common notion that rhetoricians should adapt their discourse to their readers or listeners was nearly anathema to him. His great rule of composition—to speak the truth—which he expressed in 1858 emphasized the autonomy and integrity of the speaker or the writer. He explained in his journal that if he were a professor of rhetoric, he would insist that his students "speak the truth, this first, this second, this third" (*J* 13:11). Earlier, in 1842, he had confided that "those authors are successful who do not write down to others, but make their own taste and judgement their audience," to which he added "it is enough that I please myself with my writing—I am then sure of an audience" (*J* 1:345). Thoreau's extreme position here suggests an unwillingness to adapt to the reader, an attitude that he also confirmed in 1854 by claiming that he preferred that his audience come to him than that he should go to them (*J* 7:79).

He also felt that his self was often diminished by his audience's behavior and attitudes. His audiences seemed to have the power to psychologically diminish him. In 1854, he saw adapting himself to his audience as preventing him from enjoying life (*J* 7:79). Somewhat later, in 1856, he confided in a letter to his friend Harrison Blake that "perhaps it always costs me

more than it comes to to lecture before a promiscuous audience. It is an irreparable injury done to my modesty even—I
become so indurated" (C, p. 461). Thoreau's self-image seemed
certainly threatened by his audiences' reactions. Thoreau, to be
sure, shared the common desire of writers and speakers for
their audiences to be more receptive or participatory. What
writer does not appreciate a good audience? Certainly his own
perception of the audience problem was partly colored by this
sensitivity. As a writer of finely crafted prose and carefully
constructed lectures, Thoreau may have hoped for active, ap-
preciative readers and listeners. Thoreau's commentary on his
audiences, however, goes far beyond this common sensitivity,
and his philosophy of audience is far more complex than a
utopian wish for an idealized audience.

In 1854, he also seemed convinced that the public wanted
only mediocrity from its writers and speakers (J 7:79). Later, in
1857, he saw his audiences as full of timid people waiting for a
mountebank to entertain them (J 9:238). Moreover, in 1858,
he claimed that lecture audiences only went to the lyceum to be
superficially entertained and to hear "a sugar plum" (J 11:327–
28). Thoreau may have been correct in his observation since
lyceum lectures were important cultural events and a form of
mass entertainment and education at a time when most adults
probably had less than a high school education. For many New
Englanders, the weekly lecture was certainly a source of entertainment.

Despite Thoreau's negative assessment of his audiences, he
developed an elaborate theory of audience in his journal of
1859, written near the end of his lecturing career. He saw a
symbiotic relationship between the writer or speaker and his or
her audience. Writers or speakers alone could not make a piece
of discourse effective; they must work together with their audiences as a team. The audience played an important role in
making a piece of discourse effective, and he tells us that
audiences must be credited for helping to make a piece successful and faulted for their role in its failure (J 12:11). Audiences, he claims, will take from a lecture "only such parts of
his lecture that are best heard" (J 12:9). Note that Thoreau
draws a distinction between hearing and listening, arguing that
good hearing on the part of the audience will help improve a
lecturer's performance. Thoreau felt that listening by itself did

not guarantee comprehension, and he suggests that listening itself is characterized by surface attention.

To provide a full picture of his philosophy of audience, I will discuss two of his longer commentaries on the topic of audience. First, in his journal of 1859 he develops the following elaborate parable of the speaker-audience relationship:

> The reader and the hearer are a team to be harnessed tandem, the poor wheel horse supporting the burden of the shafts, while the leader runs pretty much at will, while the lecture lies passive in the painted curricle behind. I saw some men unloading molasses-hogsheads from a truck at the depot the other day, rolling them up an inclined plane. The truckman stood behind and shoved, after putting a couple of ropes one round each end of the hogshead, while two men standing in the depot steadily pulled at the ropes. The first man was the lecturer, the last was the audience. It is the duty of the lecturer to team his hogshead of sweets to the depot, or Lyceum, place the horse, arrange the ropes, and shove; and it is the duty of the audience to take hold of the ropes and pull with all their might. The lecturer who tries to read his essay without being abetted by a good hearing is in the predicament of a teamster who is engaged in the Sisyphean labor of rolling a molasses-hogshead up an inclined plane alone, while the freight-master and his men stand indifferent with their hands in their pockets. I have seen many a hogshead which had rolled off the horse and gone to smash, with all its sweets wasted on the ground between the truckman and the freight-house, and the freight-masters thought that the loss was not theirs.
>
> Read well! Did you ever know a full well that did not yield of its refreshing waters to those who put their hands to the windlass or the well-sweep? Did you ever suck cider through a straw? Did you ever know the cider to push out of the straw when you were not sucking,—unless it chanced to be in a complete ferment? An audience will draw out of a lecture, or enable a lecturer to read, only such parts of his lecture as they like. A lecture is like a barrel half full of some palatable liquor. You may tap it at various levels,—in the sweet liquor or in the froth or in the fixed air above. If it is pronounced good it is partly to the credit of the hearers; if bad, it is partly their fault. Sometimes a lazy audience refuses to cooperate and pull on the ropes with a will, simply because the hogshead is full and therefore heavy, when if it were empty, or had only a little sugar adhering to it, they would whisk it up the slope in a jiffy. The lecturer, therefore, desires of his audience a long pull, a strong pull, and all pull together. I have seen a sturdy truckman, or lecturer, who had nearly broken his back with shoving his lecture up such an inclined plane while the audience were laughing at him, at length, as

with a last effort, set it a-rolling in amid the audience and upon their toes, scattering them like sheep and making them cry out with pain, while he drove proudly away. Rarely it is a heavy freight of such hogsheads stored in a vessel's hold that is to be lifted out and deposited on the public wharf, and this is accomplished only after many a hearty pull all together and a good deal of heave-yo-ing. [*J* 12:9–11]

This is a push-pull approach to the role of the audience in which the speaker or writer pushes his work before the listeners or readers, and the audience is expected to mentally extract meaning; that is, they are expected to pay close attention, to dig, and probe the material. Here is a notion of an active audience that would be dynamic, alert, and willing to participate in the making of meaning. The reader or listener helps to create the lecture's meaning. What is more, Thoreau clearly calls for a dynamic relationship between text and audience and, in effect, for a kind of implicit contract between the discourser and the audience in which both parties agree to perform certain duties. Thoreau, moreover, also wrote for the sort of audience that he describes here, expecting the readers of *Walden,* for example, to participate in his discourse.

Thoreau explicitly described his ideal readers in the second major passage I wish to discuss. He tells us in the "Reading" chapter of *Walden* that people read only superficially "to serve a paltry convenience, as they have learned to cipher in order to keep accounts and not be cheated in trade."[10]

Thoreau also felt that people knew little of his ideal of reading as "noble intellectual exercise" that readers must "devote our most alert and wakeful hours to" (*W,* p. 104), and he criticizes the popular romances of his time from this point of view. The formula fiction of his day, which discouraged his ideal type of reading, he satirically symbolized by the title "the Skip of the Tip-Toe-Hop, A Romance of the Middle Ages by the celebrated author of Tittle-Tol-Tan" (*W,* pp. 104–5). Thoreau's point in this chapter is that reading formula fiction is a passive, uncreative and nonparticipatory form of reading. He tells us, moreover, that the result of reading such predictable discourse is "dullness of sight, a stagnation of the vital circulations, and a general deliquirum [*sic*] and sloughing off of all the intellectual faculties" (*W,* p. 105). He also felt that such reading was unfortunately the norm for his time (*W,* p. 105).

While Thoreau often denied the need to ingratiate himself

with his audience, he sometimes expressed a begrudging acceptance of audience adaptation in his later journals. He speaks in 1855 of bending to his audience as a mere compliment which he pays them (*J* 7:197). Although he uses the word *mere*, it is a compliment nevertheless. While he was revising *Walden* in 1852, he expressed in a letter to Thomas Higginson the fear that his lectures would not "entertain a large audience, though I have thoughts to offer which I think will be quite worthy of their attention." Further on in the letter, he consents to deliver a new lecture because "the prospect of earning a few dollars is alluring" (*C*, pp. 278–79). Here I detect a conciliatory note and some willingess to bend toward an audience.

In 1854, the year that *Walden* was published, Thoreau associated rhetoric with the process of identification. He claimed that he could suit his audiences better if he suited himself less, declaring that "you cannot interest them except as you are like them and sympathize with them" (*J* 7:79). Here I think is an early version of the notion of rhetoric as identification that Kenneth Burke later developed in his *Rhetoric of Motives*. According to Burke, we persuade an audience insofar as we speak their language in idiom, syntax, imagery, and rhythm.[11]

In Thoreau's thinking on audience, there is clearly a strong bias toward seeing honest self-expression as more important than adaption to audience. In the conflict between the integrity of the self and the needs of the audience, Thoreau strongly favors the primacy of the self, a bias that reflects the basic American transcendentalist notion that the self is the center of consciousness, interpretation, and understanding. His weak concessions to his audiences seem to be the product of intensely practical needs. This rhetorical self that stands against audience adaptation is similar to Quentin Anderson's concept of the imperial self that he perceptively describes in *The Imperial Self*. Anderson's concept of the imperial self provides a valid and instructive way to view Thoreau's tendency to reject the needs of audience. He sees the imperial self as a type of "imaginative desocialization"[12] and as a way of turning away from society that Emerson bequeathed to Thoreau, to the American transcendentalist movement, and to American culture. In his essays, Emerson gave this concept of the self voice and form although this notion of the self may have existed in some form in American culture before Emerson. The individualism of the imperial self, moreover, was not the type that built American capitalism, but instead judged society to be irrelevant to human purposes, while it also stressed the importance of individual power.[13] What is more, it was a secular incarnation of divinity. Anderson explains that this self embodied the notion that individuals were "God's voice on earth" while it also stressed that true authority resided within the individual.[14]

We can, through Anderson's approach, view Thoreau's rhetorical self as antisocial and as another example of the American romantic impulse to turn inward and see the invididual as the measure of all things. Thoreau's rejection of audience considerations is fundamentally antisocial in nature. To a degree greater than we may wish to admit, Thoreau didn't care very much what his audiences thought. He didn't write to please his readers or speak to please his listeners except when he truly needed income. He often did not say what his audiences wished to hear, but he did at times create ingratiating personas to which his audiences might be drawn. He wanted *Walden* to sell well, and he must have learned a hard lesson from the poor reader reaction to *A Week on the Concord and Merrimack Rivers*.

Thoreau's history as a lecturer and his comments on audience suggest that he was a writer caught between the worlds of oral and written discourse. To an extent that we often lose sight of today, oral and written rhetoric were closely connected in America throughout most of the nineteenth century. To be sure, Thoreau moved somewhat awkwardly between the lecture platform and the world of writing. His relationship with audiences was thus profoundly different than that of most late-twentieth-century writers. His audiences must have had a strong presence for him. He commonly would have heard their reactions to his lectures, and these reactions may have been instrumental in helping him shape lectures into his published writings. He seems, nevertheless, to be caught between the worlds of oral and print literacy, and I think that his weak oral delivery skills attest to this. As I mentioned earlier, his oral style was not effective since he seldom removed his eyes from the printed page as he read his lectures. In addition, many of his written works, like the "Economy" chapter of *Walden*, exhibit an oral quality that reflects their earlier lecture origins. Thoreau seems to have struggled with a rhetorical identity crisis. Was he a writer? an orator? or was he both? Certainly his experiences as a lecturer were critical to his development as a writer.

Thoreau's approach to audience must also be seen as anticlassical. He stands clearly against the classical emphasis on adapting discourse to the needs and biases of audiences to more effectively persuade or move them. Certainly, he must have been aware of this emphasis in classical rhetoric since he was widely read in the classical Greek and Roman texts. While the rhetoricians that were studied at Harvard during his college years (1833–37)—George Campbell and Richard Whately—offered students very little guidance on audience theory, the classical approach to audience adaptation was still embodied in public discourse, in pulpit oratory, and in political discourse. In fact, Edward Tyrell Channing, the Boylston Professor of Rhetoric and Oratory at Harvard during Thoreau's student years, dropped his own emphasis on classical rhetoric from his teaching in 1832, only two years before Thoreau entered that university, by dropping Hugh Blair's *Lectures in Rhetoric and Belles Lettres,* a popular neoclassical text, in favor of Campbell's *Philosophy of Rhetoric* and Whately's *Elements of Rhetoric.*[15] Thoreau had also studied Cicero at Harvard in his Latin course,[16] and he owned a copy of Cicero's *Orationes,*[17] which certainly reflected the classical approach to audience. While Aristotle, in his *Rhetoric,* urged the rhetorician to consider the audience's biases, needs, attitudes, and politics in shaping discourse,[18] Thoreau felt that such behavior only cheapened the writer or speaker.

Let me now identify the central elements of Thoreau's thoughts on audience. First and most importantly, Thoreau believed that the expression of the self is more important than the concerns of audience. The honest expression of the writer's or speaker's message or point of view is more significant in the art of writing or speaking than the sensibilities, attitudes, or political biases of an audience. Second, he believed that adapting one's discourse, except in minimal ways, to an audience is demeaning to the writer or speaker, and doing so can only diminish the discourser's integrity. Third, Thoreau thought that audiences should be active participants in the discourse they are listening to or reading. They should not be passive but instead should actively participate with the speaker or writer in the making of meaning. They should probe, question, listen carefully, and work as partners with the speaker or writer, who should, in essence, not do the audience's thinking for them.

Thoreau's philosophy of audience, with its emphasis on the importance of the truth-telling self, also seems to be surprisingly modern. It suggests the contemporary concern with the importance of the writer's personal voice in writing theory, a concern that holds that this personal voice is the most important quality in helping us to recognize distinctive and excellent writing. Thoreau provides us with a philosophy of audience that emphasizes individualism, self-reliance, and a separateness from the attitudes of communities of listeners or readers. In this approach to rhetoric, there would be no need for demographic analysis of audience or the use of schemes or analytical systems for adapting discourse to listeners or readers. With its emphasis on self over community, Thoreau's philosophy of audience also has a romantic bias.

Notes

1. Rhetoricians have long been concerned with theories of adapting discourse to diverse audiences. Historically, rhetoricians have encouraged writers and speakers to adapt their discourse to their hearers or readers and to consider the needs, biases, and demographics of their audiences. Aristotle, for example, devoted large sections of his *Rhetoric* to advice for helping speakers appeal effectively to diverse audiences. Contemporary rhetoricians also devote considerable attention to helping writers analyze their audiences by providing such things as checklists of their audience's backgrounds, beliefs, and values and by providing elaborate heuristics and sets of questions that writers might ask about their audiences. For examples of some contemporary approaches to audience see Frank D'Angelo, *Process and Thought in Composition,* 2d ed. (Cambridge, Mass: Winthrop Publishers, 1980), p. 22, or Leonard Podis and Joanne Podis, *Writing: Invention, Form, and Style* (Glenview, Ill.: Scott, Foresman, 1984), pp. 24–34.

2. Thoreau's Harvard education in rhetoric did not offer much advice on the audience question. Thoreau's rhetoric professor, Edward Tyrell Channing, gave him rather general advice on audience typified by the notion that the best way to communicate with an audience was by being precise and avoiding such things as needless circumlocution and superfluity. See Edward T. Channing, *Lectures Read to The Seniors in Harvard College,* ed. Dorothy Anderson and Waldo Braden (Carbondale: Southern Illinois University Press, 1968), p. 236. Much of Channing's writing on audience was primarily concerned with pulpit oratory and the audience relationships of preacher to believing parishioners. He believed that the preacher was exempt from the need to answer on the spot for what he says and that he can assume that most of his hearers will listen until the end of his sermons (pp. 134–46). George Campbell and Richard Whately, the two rhetoricians studied at Harvard in Thoreau's time, had little to say on audiences as people in particular but presented instead a general theory of readers and listeners. In its simplest terms, they held that the best way to influence audience was to make your discourse perspicuous, lively, and energetic. See George Campbell, *The Philosophy of Rhetoric,* ed. Lloyd Bitzer (Carbondale: Southern Illinois University Press, 1969), pp. 71–95, and Richard Whately, *The Elements of Rhetoric,* ed. Douglas Ehninger (Carbondale: Southern Illinois University Press, 1969), Part II and Part III. Thoreau

appears to have developed his own philosophy of audience independently of the small amount of audience theory that he may have encountered.

3. Walter Harding, *The Days of Henry Thoreau: A Biography* (New York: Dover, 1982), p. 211.

4. Henry David Thoreau, *The Journal of Henry David Thoreau*, ed. Bradford Torrey and Francis H. Allen, 14 vols. (New York: Dover, 1962), 1:413; hereafter *J,* with volume and page numbers cited in the text. All citations from Thoreau's *Journal* are from this edition.

5. Harding, *Days of Thoreau,* p. 282.

6. Ibid., pp. 393–94.

7. Henry David Thoreau, *The Correspondence of Henry David Thoreau,* ed. Carl Bode and Walter Harding (New York: New York University Press, 1958), pp. 515–16; hereafter *C,* with page numbers cited in the text.

8. William Ellery Channing, *Thoreau: The Poet Naturalist,* ed. F B. Sanborn (1902; reprint ed., New York: Biblo and Tannen, 1966), p. 4.

9. Harding, *Days of Thoreau,* p. 346.

10. Henry David Thoreau, *The Illustrated Walden,* ed. J. Lyndon Shanley, Center for the Editions of American Authors edition (Princeton, N.J.: Princeton University Press, 1973), p. 104; hereafter *W,* with page numbers cited in the text.

11. Kenneth Burke, *A Rhetoric of Motives* (Berkeley: University of California Press, 1969), pp. 55–56.

12. Quentin Anderson, *The Imperial Self: An Essay in American Literary and Cultural History* (New York: Knopf, 1971), p. 4.

13. Ibid.

14. Ibid., pp. 25–35.

15. Richard H. Dillman, "Thoreau's Harvard Education in Rhetoric and Composition: 1833–1837," *Thoreau Journal Quarterly* 13 (1981):49–61.

16. Kenneth Cameron, *Thoreau's Harvard Years* (Hartford, Conn.: Transcendental Books, 1967), pp. 14–16.

17. Walter Harding, *Thoreau's Library* (Charlottesville: University of Virginia Press, 1957), p. 41.

18. Aristotle, *The Rhetoric of Aristotle,* trans. Lane Cooper (Englewood Cliffs, N.J.: Prentice-Hall, 1960), pp. 90–141.

Thoreau's Philosophy of Style

Richard H. Dillman

St. Cloud State University

HENRY David Thoreau thought extensively about the rhetorical topic of style, writing frequently about this subject in his journals, in his correspondence, and in several of his essays. His thoughts on style comprise part of a larger theory of rhetoric he recorded during the twenty-four years he kept a journal. Thoreau developed a philosophy of rhetorical invention, wrote extensively about the writer's problem of adapting discourse to his or her audience, and laid down a coherent body of thought on such areas of style as word choice, sentence form, tone, simplicity and sincerity in writing, and what he saw as the ornamental style. He also theorized about the meaning of style as a concept that both intrigued and repelled him. In his journals, correspondence, and occasionally in some of his essays, he developed a coherent philosophy of style that is important for several reasons. First, it may help us understand Thoreau's own practice and attitudes toward both his writing and that of others. Second, it may help us understand basic transcendentalist thinking about style, and, third, it comprises a significant part of his philosophy of rhetoric we are now beginning to understand. His philosophy of style is a major component of nineteenth-century American thinking about rhetoric. In this essay, I propose to examine and interpret his philosophy of style as he developed it primarily in his journals and to a lesser extent in his correspondence and other works.[1]

Thoreau clearly thought about style in terms of the options or choices available to a writer, and he frequently referred to the range of sentence types and rhetorical strategies possible for writers. Among these options he includes such things as loose sentences, periodic sentences, florid style, sincere style, concrete language, and abstract diction—typical rhetorical techniques of his time. My discussion of Thoreau's philosophy of style is based on the notion of style as a pattern of rhetorical choices governed by such things as the writer's purpose and stance toward his or her audience. Finally, I must emphasize that Thoreau's thoughts on style were remarkably consistent throughout the time that he kept his journal.[2]

Thoreau clearly thought of style in dialectical terms, often distinguishing between elements of style that stand in clear opposition to each other such as plain style versus florid or ornamental style or simple, direct sentences versus sonorous periodic sentences. He opposed the Ciceronian notion of style as ornament inherited from the eighteenth century and embodied in such neoclassical texts as Hugh Blair's *Lectures on Rhetoric and Belles Lettres* (1783) and John Quincy Adams's *Lectures on Rhetoric and Oratory* (1810). This notion of style implied that ideas exist wordlessly and can be dressed in a variety of forms to fit different occasions or audiences. As an approach to style, it stressed the use of rhetorical figures and schemes as well as verbal decoration or display. For example, in 1847 Thoreau explains that men write in a florid style because they prefer to be misunderstood[3] and that style is "something for use, and not to look at."[4]

In 1852, he asks this question: "Suppose that an equal ado were made about the ornaments of style in literature (as in architecture), should we be any more likely to attain to a truely beautiful and forcible style?" He explains further that "I do not believe that any writer who considered the ornaments and not the truth simply, ever succeeded" (*J* 3:278–79). He definitely prefers the plain style that flowed, he believed, from great or important points. "Plain speech is always a desideratum" (*J* 1:342–43), he tells us in 1842. The true ornaments of style, he continues, are "plainness, vigor, and sincerity," and these are "better learned on the farm and in the workshops than in the schools."[5]

He emphasized, moreover, that thought precedes style. The effective writer or speaker will not know his style before writing, but will find instead that great thoughts may lead to effective style. In 1842, he tells us that "it is the style of thought entirely and not the style of expression which makes the difference in books" (*J* 1:344). He also explains that "the question for us is not whether Pope had a fine style, wrote with a

Peacock's feather, but whether he uttered useful thoughts" (*EE*, p.232). "Translate a book a dozen times from one language to another and what becomes of its style?" he asks in 1847. "Most books would be worn out and disappear in this ordeal" (*EE*, p.232).

He also preferred that a writer's style be as intelligible as his thought, claiming that style is "not worth scraping and polishing and gilding unless it will write his thoughts the better for it" (*EE*, p.232). Later, in 1851, he tells us that "a genuine thought or feeling can find expression for itself, if it have to invent hieroglyphics. . . . It is for want of original thought that one man's style is like another's" (*J* 2:480). He clearly felt that the message was more important than the style, and he saw effective thinking as a prerequisite for effective style.

In his emphasis on the plain and sincere style, Thoreau also identified a connection between style and physical labor. Manual labor, he tells us, is the best way to remove "palaver out of one's style" (*J* 1:312–13). The writer will avoid ornament when he has wood to cut in the short days of winter. The scholar will write "the tougher truth for the calluses on his palms" which will give "firmness to the sentence. Indeed, the mind never makes a great and successful effort, without a corresponding energy of the body." He goes on to write that "we are often struck by the force and precision of style to which hard working men, unpracticed in writing, easily attain when required to make the effort" (*W*, pp.105–7). This is the basis of a populist approach to style that emphasizes the language of the commoner and laborer against the seemingly effete language of the scholar.

I will next discuss and examine two specific aspects of Thoreau's philosophy of style: his thoughts on word choice and his thoughts on sentence form. Thoreau was fascinated with the power of words and expressed sensitivity to the impact that certain types of words had on readers and listeners. In his journals, he discussed three aspects of word choice that I will examine here: brevity or conciseness in choice of words, words derived from nature and popular speech, and the disadvantages of abstract and technical terms.

Thoreau favored brevity and conciseness, telling us that a small compass of words would suggest many: "By your few words show how insufficient would be many words."[6] Later, in 1852, he tells us that writers should follow nature because she is a plain writer who uses few gestures, and, in the same passage, he indicates his own practice in struggling with wordiness in the following candid admission: "I find that I use many words for the sake of emphasis which really add nothing to the force of my sentences, and they look relieved the moment I have cancelled these. Words by which I express my mood, my conviction, rather than the simple truth" (*J* 3:233). Words should be well-chosen and economical in the sense that they suggest much—"In breadth we may be patterns of conciseness, but in depth we may well be prolix" (CEAA 1:194), he tells us in 1840.

He was also fascinated by suggestive sounding names because "they strike the fancy and suggest ideas in harmony with the flower" (*J* 4:154, in 1852). Moreover, he saw the art of naming things as poetic when he extolled a tree called the wayfarer's tree: "The mass of men are very unpoetic, yet that Adam that names things is always a poet. The boor is ready to accept the name the poet gives. How nameless is the poet among us!" (*J* 5:347, in 1853). Thoreau also tells us that when choosing words we should follow nature whenever possible. He clarified this position at length in his journal of 1860:

> As in the expression of moral truths we admire any closeness to the physical fact which in all language is the symbol of the spiritual, so, finally, when natural objects are described, it is an advantage if words derived originally from nature, it is true, but which have turned (tropes) from their primary signification to a moral sense, are used, i.e., if the object is personified. The one who loves and understands a thing the best will incline to use the personal pronouns in speaking of it. To him there is no *neuter* gender. Many of the words of the old naturalists were in this sense double tropes. [*J* 13:145–46]

This is a transcendentalist notion of word choice, with its emphasis on physical facts symbolizing the spiritual. Facts expressed in concrete language suggest larger themes and ideas. Here Thoreau emphasizes using personification to describe natural objects since the vehicle for this trope will be more concrete than the tenor. In another important passage in 1859, he tells us that natural objects and phenomena are the original symbols or types which express our thoughts and feelings (*J* 12:389–90), an idea that he links to a critique of American scholars striving to employ British usage or "imported symbols," thereby rejecting the "living speech" of their country as

"Americanisms" (J 12:389–90). He thus exhorts us to originate our own words out of American experiences and a more intimate and deeper knowledge of life.

Thoreau also felt that popular phrasing was admirable and preferable to formal language or the hard technical language of science and technology. He explains that the "value of any statement may be measured by its susceptibility to be expressed in popular language," and "the greatest discoveries," he tells us, "can be reported in the newspapers" (J 3:327–28, in 1852). What is more, he explains that in the life of the western frontier there is a new source of picturesque language that is tied to the soil and may "now look raw and slang-like and colloquial" but "when printed another generation will cherish and affect as genuine American and standard" (CEAA 1:481, in 1843).

Thoreau was also against using dry technical language or specialized jargon. When reporting on his reaction to the reports of scientific meetings, he tells us that he is "put off with a parcel of dry technical terms," and he speculates that the lives of academics who use such language are "almost as inhuman and wooden as a rain gauge or self-regulating magnetic machine that communicates no fact which rises to the temperature of blood heat" (J 6:237–38, in 1854). Moreover, he saw scientific terms as hiding the reality of their referents like a mask: "Whatever aid is to be derived from the use of a scientific term, we can never begin to see anything as it is so long as we remember the scientific term which always our ignorance has imposed on it. Natural objects and phenomena are in this sense forever wild and unnamed by us" (J 13:141, in 1860). He does, however, see one advantage to using scientific jargon—the task of learning such language can help make us better informed about science (J 3:326, in 1852).

Thoreau's views on abstract language are similar to his views on technical language. He saw highly abstract, academic language as lifeless and arid, telling us that "a writer who does not speak out of full experience uses torpid words, wooden or lifeless words, such words as 'humanitary,' which have a paralysis in their tails" (J 4:225, in 1852).

On word choice, Thoreau clearly favors brevity, concreteness, and the language of the common people except in certain circumstances. He prefers language that is concrete, deeply rooted in experience, and suggestive in part because it brings us closer to nature. He essentially rejects academic abstractions and technical jargon as lifeless, dull, and capable of obscuring the subject matter of discourse. In essence, such language acts as a mask that hides the reality behind the surface of the phrasing. In true transcendentalist fashion, he sees such language as a curtain that obscures deeper realities. Let me now turn to his thoughts on sentence structure, another important aspect of his philosophy of style.

Thoreau's philosophy of sentence structure is quite complex. He does not speak of grammatical sentence types, and he argues effectively against the periodic form inherited from the neoclassical period and the eighteenth century. He asks us "Who is not tired of the weak and flowing periods of the politician and scholar, and resorts not even to the Farmer's Almanac to read the simple account of the month's labor, to restore his tone again?" (*J* 1:313, in 1842.) He argues instead for sentences that are simple and suggestive. His plain sentences would have "the strength and compactness of masonry" and would be composed of words that were "sufficiently simple and answering to the thing to be expressed." In sentences, at least, he tells us that "simplicity is exuberant" (*J* 1:343, in 1842). To Thoreau, the sentence is a true work of art that should be composed with great care. It is "a diamond found in the sand, or a pearl fished out of the sea" (*J* 1:350, in 1842). "A perfectly healthy sentence is extremely rare," he explains, and "the most attractive sentences are the surest and roundest" (*EE*, p. 214, in 1843).

Much of his commentary on sentences explains aphoristic and sententious sentence form. To illustrate this idea, I will list Thoreau's comments on this sentence type in the order in which he expressed them:

I want to see a sentence run clear through to the end, as deep and fertile as a well-drawn furrow which shows that the plow was pressed down to the beam. [*J* 1:313, in 1842]

A well-built sentence, in the rapidity and force with which it works, may be compared to a modern cornplanter, which furrows out, drops the seed, and covers it up at one movement. [*J* 1:313, in 1842]

It is the fault of some excellent writing—DeQuincy's first impressions on seeing London suggest it to me—that they express themselves with too great fullness and detail. They give the most faithful, natural, and lifelike account of their sensations, mental and physical, but they lack moderation and sententiousness. They do not affect us by an ineffectual earnestness and a reserve of meaning, like a stutterer; they say all they mean. Their sentences are not concentrated and nutty. Sentences which suggest far more than they say, which have an atmosphere about them, which do not merely report an old, but make a new, impression: sentences which suggest as many things and are as durable as a Roman aqueduct; to frame these, that is the *art* of writing. Sentences which are expensive, towards which so many volumes, so much life, went; which lie like boulders on the page, up and down or across; which contain the seed of other sentences, not mere repetition, but creation; which a man might sell his grounds and castles to build. [*J* 2:418–19, in 1851]

The writer must direct his sentences as carefully and leisurely as the marksman his rifle, who shoots sitting and with a rest, with patent sights and conical balls beside. He must not merely seem to speak the truth. He must really speak it. [*J* 3:230–31, in 1851]

New ideas come into this world somewhat like falling meteors, with a flash and an explosion, and perhaps somebody's castle roof perforated. To try to polish the stone in its descent, to give it a peculiar turn and make it whistle a tune perchance, would be of no use, if it were possible.[7]

The themes of rapidity and force, of rapid impact, of suggestiveness, are apparent throughout this commentary. Important terms include "deep and fertile," "rapidity and force," the sentence as a "seed," "concentrated and nutty," "boulders on the page," "falling meteors," and the marksman metaphor of the fourth passage. Thoreau's ideal sentences would be compact with meaning, suggesting far more than they say, and they would prompt us to think in new ways. They would also be relatively brief, yet their meanings might echo in our minds for a long time. They would, in a metaphoric sense, plant seeds that would promote further thought. Who knows what additional ideas might develop from these sentences? Here then is the theoretical basis for a specific type of rhetorical sentence that is loosely categorized under the concept of sententia that would include the aphorism, the maxim, and aphoristic paradoxes. Here too is the theoretical explanation for Thoreau's own frequent use of aphoristic sentences that are both thought provoking and forceful. The following sentences from *Walden* are typical of this rhetorical pattern:

The mass of men lead lives of quiet desperation. [P. 8]

But lo! We have become the tools of their tools. [P. 37]

I have learned that the swiftest traveler is he that goes afoot. [P. 53]

We are determined to be starved before we are hungry. [P. 93]

Such forceful sentences require the power of a speaker or writer with integrity to stand behind them. These are sentences, he tells us, that are "spoken firmly and conclusively as if the author had a right to know what he says; and if not wise, they have at least been well learned. At least he does not stand on a rolling stone, but is well assured of his footing—and if you dispute their doctrine you will yet allow that there is truth in their assurance" (*EE*, p.214, in 1843). Moreover, in his journal of 1845, Thoreau calls for the aphoristic sentence to be treated as a true work of art: "The choicest maxims that have come down to us are more beautiful or integrally wise than they are wise to our understandings. This wisdom which we are inclined to pluck from the stalk is the point only of a single association. Every natural form—palm leaves and acorns, oak leaves and sumach and dodder—are [*sic*] untranslatable aphorisms" (*J* 1:380). Thus he views the aphorism as capable of imitating the suggestive power of nature.

The forceful sentence type that Thoreau preferred stands in stark contrast to the classical periodic sentence with its balanced phrasing, its step by step progression, and its climactic arrangement that urges us to suspend our thoughts to the very end. He felt that his peers were tired of the "weak and flowing periods of the politician and scholar" (*J* 1:313, in 1842). In rejecting the periodic sentence, Thoreau does not reject the need for sentence rhythm, and he calls instead for a natural rhythm that suggests life, growth, and additional thought. "There is a true march to the sentence," he explains, "as if a man or a body of men were actually making progress there step by step, and these are not mere *disjecta membra*, the dispersed and mutilated members though it were of heroes, which can no longer join themselves to their comrades" (*J* 1:480, about 1842). If I interpret this correctly, Thoreau criticizes the periodic sentence of political oratory, which he sees as consisting partly of too many seemingly unconnected clauses and phrases (i.e., members).

Thoreau also discussed the connection between grammar and style. He denigrated the role of grammar in writing, claiming that the prescriptive grammarians "forget that the first requisite and rule is that expression be vital and natural, as much as the voice of a brute or an interjection: first of all, mother tongue; and last of all, artificial or father tongue" (*J* 11:386). Moreover, another comment on grammar and writing appears to be cutting and overstated. For example, when he reads some of the rules for speaking and writing correctly, he thinks that "Any fool can make a rule / And any fool will mind it" (*J* 13 : 125, in 1860).

Thoreau's preferred writing style, then, would be grounded in fact. Details would be factual, concrete, and specific. There would be a strong sense that discourse was tied to the natural world and its images. Facts would be larger than themselves; they would be mythologic and significant, suggesting more abstract notions. He tells, moreover, that "facts should only be as the frame to my pictures; they should be material to the mythology which I am writing . . . facts to tell who I am, and where I have been or what I have thought" (*J* 3:99, in 1851). He will state his facts in such a way that they will be significant (*J* 3:99). These are facts used in the manner of the synecdoche, where the part suggests the whole or the concrete suggests the abstract and the mythologic. This rhetorical strategy is also common in Thoreau's own prose.

He was an organicist on style, believing that style often derived from thought. The writer's most important task was to discover and effectively write the truth. The style would follow but not precede the truth. Subject would be more important than ornament or decoration. He clearly reacted against the neoclassical idea of style as ornament, which he certainly would have known since this approach to style was still current in the Boston area during Thoreau's college years. The Ciceronian approach of style was deleted from the Harvard curriculum in 1830, two years before Thoreau entered Harvard, by Edward Tyrell Channing when he dropped Hugh Blair's *Lectures in Rhetoric and Belles Lettres* in favor of George Campbell's *Philosophy of Rhetoric* and Richard Whately's *Elements of Rhetoric*.[8] Thoreau also owned a copy of Cicero's *Orationes*, a text that typified the ornate style.[9]

Thoreau clearly favored a plain style that reflects the vocabulary and rhythms of popular speech. We might even call this emphasis in his philosophy of style populist. In his journals, for example, he refers to the speaking or writing styles of laborers or farmers in very positive ways, as the following examples illustrate:

I have often been astonished at the force and precision of style to which busy laboring men, unpracticed in writing, easily attain when they are required to make the effort. [*J* 1:313, in 1842]

The scholar not infrequently envies the propriety and emphasis with which the farmer calls to his team, and confesses that if that lingo were written it would surpass his labored sentences. [*J* 1:313, in 1842]

On word choice he clearly emphasized the concrete and specific and words derived from nature. He rejected abstractions and the overuse of jargon and scientific language because such phrasing often masked reality. Moreover, he favored words derived from nature that have their roots in the soil of everyday experience. In this romantic view, these words can surely be symbols for larger, spiritual truths. Moreover, his notion of sentence form is clearly populist in its emphasis on the terse and laconic forms the laboring men used, if we reason that the rural New England dialect of his day was the model for Thoreau's thinking here. His emphasis on the aphoristic sentence form, too, places the stress on conciseness, brevity, and integrity. He preferred direct, assertive, honest sentences. He felt that wordy sentences and convoluted sentences would only weaken a writer's style. His bias here is clearly anti-Ciceronian and against the notion of style as ornament.

Thoreau clearly takes a romantic, transcendentalist approach to style. In his view, the honest writer or speaker would be concerned with the truth first, and the appropriate expression of the writer's subject would take precedence over artifice and the ornaments of style. Such a style would seem natural and partake of colloquial rhetoric, drawing its rhythms from the speech of farmers, laborers, and the new settlers on the Western frontier. It would clearly not draw its inspiration from the speech or writing of the British upper classes, from polite literature, or from political oratory. It is basically an unpretentious, populist approach to style. It is organic, too, in the sense that a writer's style would grow from the thought, while thought would precede and strongly influence the development of the style.

Style, in this approach, is also linked to rhetorical invention or the art of discovering ideas for writing or speaking. If, in an act of writing, ideas are discovered as the writing progresses, then this discovery will influence the emergent style. Under such an approach, planning the writer's style would prove futile. In an 1851 discussion of the problems of discovering material for writing, Thoreau wrote that "a man must see before he can say" (*J* 3:85).

Notes

1. For discussion of Thoreau's rhetorical strategies and practice, see Richard Dillman, "The Psychological Rhetoric of *Walden*," *ESQ: A Journal of the American Renaissance* 25 (1979): 79–91 and Joseph Moldenhauer, "Paradox in *Walden*," *Twentieth-Century Interpretations of Walden*, ed. Richard Ruland (Englewood Cliffs, N. J.: Prentice-Hall, 1968), pp. 73–84. For discussion of Thoreau's education in rhetoric, see Richard Dillman, "Thoreau's Harvard Education in Rhetoric and Composition: 1833–1837," *Thoreau Journal Quarterly* 13 (1981): 49–61. Finally, for discussions of possible influences on Thoreau's thinking about language, see Phillip Gura, "Language and Meaning: An American Tradition," *American Literature* 53 (1981): 1–21 and Michael West, "Thoreau and the Language Theories of the French Enlightenment," *Journal of English Literary History* 51 (1984): 747–70.

2. Thoreau's recorded thoughts on style are consistent throughout his life as a writer. At different periods of his career, he discussed different aspects of style, often leaving one topic to proceed to another. His later comments on style sometimes amplify his earlier commentary, and he does not contradict his earlier views on style.

3. Henry David Thoreau, *The Journal of Henry David Thoreau*, ed. Bradford Torrey and Francis H. Allen, 14 vols. (New York: Dover, 1962), 1:342–43; hereafter *J*, with volume and page numbers cited in the text. All citations from Thoreau's *Journal* are from this edition unless otherwise noted.

4. Henry David Thoreau, *Early Essays and Miscellanies*, ed. Joseph Moldenhauer (Princeton, N. J.: Princeton University Press, 1975), p. 232; hereafter *EE*, with page numbers cited in the text.

5. Henry David Thoreau, *A Week on the Concord and Merrimack Rivers*, in *Walden*, ed. J. Lyndon Shanley (Princeton, N. J.: Princeton University Press, 1971), pp. 105–7; hereafter *W*, with page numbers cited in the text.

6. Henry David Thoreau, *Journal. Volume 1: 1832–1844*, ed. John C. Broderick et al. (Princeton, N. J.: Princeton University Press, 1981), 1:194. Hereafter CEAA will be used to identify this Center for the Editions of American Authors edition of the journal, which, at the present time, is complete only through volume 2.

7. Henry David Thoreau, *The Correspondence of Henry David Thoreau*, ed. Carl Bode and Walter Harding (New York: New York University Press, 1958), p. 489; the date for this quotation is 1857.

8. Dillman, "Thoreau's Harvard Education," pp. 50–51.

9. Walter Harding, *Thoreau's Library* (Charlottesville: University of Virginia Press, 1957), p. 41.

Madness and Right Reason, Extremes of One: The Shadow Archetype in *Moby-Dick*

Michael Vannoy Adams

New School for Social Research

IF Ahab's conflict with the fish archetype in *Moby-Dick* defines the terms of his Jonah-and-the-Whale complex,[1] his confrontation with the shadow archetype[2] provides an explanation for his attraction to and fascination with evil. The shadow archetype, Jung says, is the individual's dark or evil side, which is denied, repressed, and projected (cast like a shadow) onto others. At dawn on the day of the *Pequod*'s departure Ishmael sees some men moving in the mist—not "shadows," he dimly surmises, but simple sailors like himself.[3] He sees nothing more of them until the voyage is well under way, when one of the crew cries out at a whale spout. The shout is so alarming that Ishmael compares the sailor to a prophet "beholding the shadows of Fate, and by those wild cries announcing their coming" (p. 186). No sooner does Ishmael make the comparison than the shadows themselves materialize. The crew eagerly rush to the rail to see the whale. "But at this critical instant," Ishmael says, "a sudden exclamation was heard that took every eye from the whale. With a start all glared at dark Ahab, who was surrounded by five dusky phantoms that seemed fresh formed out of air" (p. 187). The shadow, Jung says, "belongs to the realm of bodiless phantoms,"[4] and so do Ahab's shadows, disembodied one instant and embodied the next. Psychologically speaking,

97

their disembodiment is equivalent to repression and their embodiment equivalent to projection. When Ahab represses his dark or evil side, the phantoms disappear; when he projects it, they reappear.

The archetype of the shadow is closely related to the archetype of the demon. "This figure," Jung says, "often appears as dark-skinned and of mongoloid type, and then it represents a negative and possibly dangerous aspect. Sometimes it can hardly be distinguished, if at all, from the shadow."[5] This is, of course, a psychological proposition about the racial prejudices of those who, like Ahab, themselves appear as light skinned and of caucasoid type. Jung is saying that in the collective unconscious of the occidental the archetype of the demon quite frequently appears as a figure with the features of an oriental. In just this way Fedallah, the only one of Ahab's shadows known by name, is dark skinned, or "swart," and is dressed in dark, Chinese cloth. The other shadows are "less swart in aspect"; they are yellow skinned. They represent "a race notorious for a certain diabolism of subtility." Some white-skinned sailors, Ishmael says, even suspect them to be "agents on the water of the devil" (p. 187). Fedallah himself exerts some vague influence, or perhaps even absolute authority, over Ahab (p. 199). The second mate takes Fedallah to be "the devil in disguise." Ahab, he says, is hell bent after Moby Dick, "and the devil there is trying to come round him, and get him to swap away . . . his soul, or something of that sort, and then he'll surrender Moby Dick" (p. 275). This is perfectly consistent with the formulation Jung presents, when he says,"the devil is a variant of the 'shadow' archetype, i.e., of the dangerous aspect of the unrecognized dark half of the personality."[6] Fedallah is, if not the devil himself, Mephistopheles to Melville's Faust, Ahab, whose soul is signed, sealed, and delivered.

According to Jung, the shadow archetype has "an obsessive or, better, possessive quality."[7] In Ahab's Jonah-and-the-Whale complex psychotic obsession is tantamount to demonic possession. Just after Ahab's relationship with Fedallah is described as a pact with the devil, Ahab chances to stand, Ishmael says, so that Fedallah "occupied his shadow" (which is to say, possessed his soul), while, if Fedallah's "shadow was there at all it seemed only to blend with, and lengthen Ahab's" (p. 278). Ahab is not the only one whose soul is possessed by the devil. All the sailors who participate in Ahab's revenge are parties to the pact:

> How it was that they so aboundingly responded to the old man's
> ire—by what evil magic their souls were possessed, that at times his
> hate seemed almost theirs; the White Whale as much their insuf-
> ferable foe as his; how all this came to be—what the White Whale
> was to them, or how to their unconscious understandings, also, in
> some dim, unsuspected way, he might have seemed the gliding
> great demon of the seas of life,—all this to explain, would be to dive
> deeper than Ishmael can go. [P. 162]

The sailors wonder whether Fedallah "were a mortal substance,
or else a tremulous shadow cast upon the deck by some unseen
being's body." Fedallah and Ahab stare at each other, Ishmael
says, as if in Fedallah Ahab "saw his forethrown shadow," and in
Ahab, Fedallah "his abandoned substance" (pp. 438–39).

Fedallah is not only Ahab's "lean shade" (p. 439) but also a
psychologist who, like Freud and Jung, interprets dreams.
Ahab is disturbed by "intolerably vivid dreams of the night"
that are directly related to his "intense thoughts through the
day." These dreams convulse his very being; a deep split develops in his personality, and from this bottomless pit flames
and lightnings flash and bolt, and fiends, damned to "this hell in
himself," impel Ahab to plunge into pandemonium. As the
abyss widens, Ahab wakes and runs panic-stricken from his
room, as if his bed were on fire. Rather than "being the unsup-
pressable symptoms of some latent weakness, or fright at his
own resolve," these nightmares are the clearest signs of Ahab's
headstrong will (p. 174). In sleep Ahab suffers a dissociation of
the conscious and the unconscious (in Melville's words, the
"mind" and the "soul"):

> The latter was the eternal, living principle or soul in him; and in
> sleep, being for the time dissociated from the characterizing mind,
> which at other times employed it for its outer vehicle or agent, it
> spontaneously sought escape from the scorching contiguity of the
> frantic thing, of which, for the time, it was no longer an integral.
> But as the mind does not exist unless leagued with the soul, there-
> fore it must have been that, in Ahab's case, yielding up all his
> thoughts and fancies to his one supreme purpose; that purpose, by
> its own sheer inveteracy of will, forced itself against gods and devils
> into a kind of self-assumed, independent being of its own. [P. 175]

Ahab has a recurrent dirge of a bad dream. Fedallah gives the
nightmare a prophetic interpretation. The dream is, literally, a
rehearsal for Ahab's death. Before Ahab can die, Fedallah says,

he must see two hearses: the one "not made by mortal hands," the other, made of wood "grown in America." If the end should come, Fedallah says that he will "go before," or die first. He also tells Ahab, "Hemp only can kill thee." Ahab ridicules the interpretation: "The gallows, ye mean.—I am immortal then, on land and on sea" (pp. 410–11).

Jung says that recurrent dreams "usually compensate a defect in one's conscious attitude, or they date from a traumatic moment that has left behind some specific prejudice, or they anticipate a future event of some importance."[8] Ahab's nightmare satisfies all of these conditions; his dream is at once a premonition and an admonition, a foreknowing and a forewarning. The dream performs a compensatory function (or it *would* perform such a function if Ahab's conscious attitude were not *so* defective) insofar as it intimates that Ahab should reverse course in order to forestall a fatal confrontation with Moby Dick. Although Ishmael does not say so, the implication is that the nightmare dates from the onset of Ahab's insanity. It is unlikely, Ishmael says, that Ahab's madness "took its instant rise at the precise time of his bodily dismemberment." It is far more likely that Ahab suffered a state of shock and at first "felt the agonizing bodily laceration, but nothing more," and that it was only on the return voyage, after his encounter with Moby Dick, that "the final monomania seized him" and left him such "a raving lunatic" that he had to be laced fast in a straitjacket (p. 160). Ahab relives the experience in his imagination in a futile effort to relieve the pain, which is not only physical but also psychical. Whatever the exact timing of Ahab's psychosis, his recurrent dream is a repetition compulsion that derives from the traumatic moment when Moby Dick devoured and swallowed his leg. His nightmare is also a prophetic anticipation of a future event of the utmost importance: his death. But the dream is just ambiguous enough (and Fedallah's interpretation just indefinite and implausible enough) that it can accommodate even the most favorable construction, and Ahab's powers of rationalization are such that he distorts the meaning to suit himself.

On the second day of the chase Fedallah is drowned, dragged down and under by Moby Dick. "In Jesus' name," the first mate says, "no more of this, that's worse than devil's madness." Fedallah, Ahab's "evil shadow," is gone (p. 459). What more does Ahab want? But Ahab refuses to abandon the chase. On the third day Moby Dick rises from the sea. The White Whale itself is the first hearse, not made of mortal hands. Lashed to the Whale's back is Fedallah's body, lacerated like Ahab's. Aye, Ahab says, "I see thee again.—Aye, and thou goest before; and this, *this* then is the hearse that thou didst promise. But I hold thee to the last letter of thy word. Where is the second hearse?" (pp. 464–65). No sooner said than done, Moby Dick staves the *Pequod*. "The ship! The hearse!—the second hearse!" Ahab exclaims; "its wood could only be American!" Ahab's bad dream comes true: "Sink all coffins and all hearses to one common pool! and since neither can be mine, let me then tow to pieces, while still chasing thee, though tied to thee, thou damned whale!" (p. 468). With that, Ahab hurls his harpoon. The rope runs foul; Ahab frees it, but the line loops like a noose around his neck and hangs him by the hemp of his own harpoon, on the gallows of his own revenge: Ahab is mortal after all.

The shadow in Ahab's Jonah-and-the-Whale complex is not only a psychological but also a moral problem. Ahab is not simply insane: he is evil. As Jung says:

> The shadow is a moral problem that challenges the whole ego-personality, for no one can become conscious of the shadow without considerable moral effort. To become conscious of it involves recognizing the dark aspects of the personality as present and real. This act is the essential condition for any kind of self-knowledge, and it therefore, as a rule, meets with considerable resistance.[9]

Ahab's resistance is especially strong because Fedallah and the other shadows are projections that exert an unconscious and therefore ungovernable influence over his ego. In such a case, Jung says, even intuition and the best of intentions are ineffectual:

> Although, with insight and good will, the shadow can to some extent be assimilated into the conscious personality, experience shows that there are certain features which offer the most obstinate resistance to moral control and prove almost impossible to influence. These resistances are usually bound up with *projections*, which are not recognized as such, and their recognition is a moral achievement beyond the ordinary. While some traits peculiar to the shadow can be recognized without too much difficulty as one's own personal qualities, in this case both insight and good will are unavailing because the cause of the emotion appears to lie, beyond all possibility of doubt, in the *other person*. No matter how obvious it may be

to the neutral observer that it is a matter of projections, there is little hope that the subject will perceive this himself. He must be convinced that he throws a very long shadow before he is willing to withdraw his emotionally-toned projections from their object.[10]

Projections, Jung says, give rise to an "autistic condition in which one dreams a world whose reality remains forever unattainable." The result is a *sentiment d'incomplétude*, which the individual explains "by projection as the malevolence of the environment."[11] In just this way Ahab dreams a whale whose reality remains forever unattainable, and the result is a pathetic sense of incompleteness, which Ahab explains by projection as the malevolence of Moby Dick.

Ahab resists the very idea that a moral effort might make any difference. He resigns himself to what he takes to be his fate. He believes that his conflict with Moby Dick is the fulfillment of a prophecy, and this fatalistic attitude relieves him of any responsibility for his actions. "By heaven, man," he says, "we are turned round and round in this world, like yonder windlass, and Fate is the handspike" (p. 445). If the end is inevitable, the means are immaterial or, in Ahab's case, immoral. Ahab refuses to recognize that Fedallah and the other shadows are the evil casts of his own character, alternately repressed and projected. He may be the *Pequod*'s captain, but he is also "the Fates' lieutenant" (p. 459), and he acts under orders from the collective unconscious. Ahab is one of those who, Jung says, "finally give up all sense of responsibility, overcome by a sense of the powerlessness of the ego against the fate working through the unconscious." But there is a paradox here, for this compliant lack of power obscures a superiority complex, "a defiant will to power." The ego inflation that accompanies such a state is, in Jung's words, a "godlikeness." The individual who likens himself to God imputes "to himself qualities or values which obviously do not belong to him, for to be 'godlike' is to be like a spirit superior to the spirit of man."[12] Ahab is just such a contradiction in terms, "a grand, ungodly, god-like man" (p. 76). His will to power over the whale is defiant and ungodly. He worships not God but the devil, whose "right worship is defiance" (p. 416). He baptizes his harpoon not in holy water but in unholy blood: *Ego non baptizo te in nomine patris, sed in nomine diaboli* (p. 404)—not in the name of the father, but in the name of the devil—which, according to Melville, is "the book's motto (the secret one)."[13]

The first mention Melville makes of his secret motto is in a letter to Nathaniel Hawthorne. In a subsequent letter Melville says, "I have written a wicked book, and feel as spotless as the lamb."[14] To take Melville at his word, and to treat *Moby-Dick* as an evil book, is to regard Ahab's devil worship as the epitome of that wickedness. For it is Ahab's evil personality or, more properly speaking, the shadow side of his character, that finds its objective correlative in the devil. The secret motto is an elliptical variant of a note penciled by Melville to himself on the flyleaf of the last volume of his set of Shakespeare:

Ego non baptizo te in nomine Patri et
Filii et Spiritus Sancti—sed in nomine
Diaboli.—madness is undefinable—
It & right reason extremes of one,
—not the (black art) Goetic but Theurgic magic—
seeks converse with the Intelligence, Power, the
Angel.[15]

The note serves as a gloss on Melville's psychological intention in *Moby-Dick*, but a gloss that itself requires interpretation. Melville places the devil in diametric opposition not only to the father but also to the son and the holy ghost. Like Jung, he regards the exclusion of the devil from the Trinity as a psychological problem. At issue is the definability of madness.

According to Jung, the Christian Trinity is psychologically incomplete. It is deficient insofar as it denies the intrinsic contrariness of God's character. God, Jung says, is a being in whom the contraries good and evil coexist as complementary or mutually compensatory aspects of a paradoxical personality. This is, of course, a radical departure from Christian tradition, which treats good and evil not as coexistent and consubstantial contraries but as outright contradictories, the one existent and substantial, the other nonexistent and insubstantial. The tradition that good and evil are mutually exclusive or logically incompatible moral terms (evil being the mere shadow of good) may be agreeable as a theological dogma, Jung says, but it is untenable as a psychological proposition. He says that "whereas the central Christian symbolism is a Trinity, the formula presented by the unconscious is a quaternity." To the theologian, God is wholly good and threefold (father, son, and holy ghost); to the analytical psychologist, he is *partly evil* and fourfold (father, son, holy ghost, *and devil*). The Christian formula, Jung says, "is not quite complete, because the dogmatic aspect of the evil principle is absent from the Trinity and leads a more or less awkward existence on its own as the devil."[16]

To deny that this aspect is present in the quaternity of the collective unconscious is to split the personality into irreconcilable opposites (good and evil, God and devil, substance and shadow) and to project the evil principle as a separate being, the devil, the shadow of the Trinity. According to Jung, the exclusion of the devil from the Trinity derives its theological justification from the *privatio boni*, which says that evil is not a real presence but the mere absence of good (only for lack of a better word does the privation of good go by the name of "evil"; theologically speaking, the rubric is a misnomer).[17] As Ralph Waldo Emerson says, "Good is positive. Evil is merely privative, not absolute. It is like cold, which is the privation of heat."[18] By denying that evil, like good, exists in its own right as an essential aspect of the personality, the *privatio boni* contradicts psychological experience, and that is why, Jung says, "psychology must insist on the reality of evil and must reject any definition that regards it as insignificant or actually non-existent."[19] Evil is an existent and an immensely significant one in Ahab's Jonah-and-the-Whale complex. But Ahab insists on the unreality of evil in himself and, as a result, he projects that aspect of his personality as a separate being, the devil, whom he dissociates from the Trinity and worships in opposition to the father, son, and holy ghost.

This split is symbolized on one level by the phantoms of Ahab's imagination. Fedallah and the other shadows are not only types of demonism, with an obsessive or possessive quality, but also prophetic anticipations of Ahab's death, the fulfillment of which is a foregone conclusion. They are also silhouettes of evil, phantasmagoric projections from Ahab's psychological profile. As Ishmael exclaims in exasperation:

> Ah, ye admonitions and warnings! why stay ye not when ye come? But rather are ye predictions than warnings, ye shadows! Yet not so much predictions from without as verifications of the foregoing things within. For with little external to constrain us, the innermost necessities in our being, these still drive us on. [P. 145]

Ahab's shadows do not stay, they come and go, for the precise reason that they exist only as projections. What is repressed within is projected without. The shadows are not so much forecasts of fate as casts of character, not so much predictions from external reality as verifications of internal reality, symbols of the psychological conflict that splits Ahab's personality into opposites. It is no outer constraint but the inner necessity of the collective unconscious that drives Ahab on, and drives him crazy.

The split in Ahab's personality is symbolized on another level by Moby Dick, who at least to Ahab is the very personification of evil. Ishmael says that "all the subtle demonisms of life and thought; all evil, to crazy Ahab, were visibly personified, and made practically assailable in Moby Dick" (p. 160). But what is to Ahab personified *in* Moby Dick is really only imputed *to* Moby Dick by Ahab. One sailor says that Ahab's dismemberment was a mere accident. He tells Ahab that "what you take for the White Whale's malice is only his awkwardness," for Moby Dick "never means to swallow a single limb" (p. 368). Ahab, however, contends that his dismemberment was not accidental but intentional, neither the inadvertent result of a lack of coordination nor an instinctive response to the stimulus of the harpoon, but an intelligent act executed with evil intent: Moby Dick *meant* to devour his leg out of sheer malice. The imputation of evil to Moby Dick is another umbrageous projection from the suggestible ego of Ahab, whose Jonah-and-the-Whale complex is a persecution complex accompanied by paranoid delusions of grandeur.

There is an astrological analogue to Ahab's psychological condition. The split in his personality parallels what Jung calls "the antagonism Christ-Antichrist, represented in the traditional zodiacal symbolism of the two fishes."[20] Ahab expects to encounter Moby Dick on the equator at the equinox, when the sign of Pisces, or the Fishes, is on the rise. This expectation is not an inference of causal logic but an instance of acausal synchronicity, an astrological coincidence with a psychological meaning.[21] When Pisces rises in the sky, Moby Dick rises in the sea and surfaces on the ocean of the collective unconscious. Jung says that there was originally one great fish, which eventually split in two to form the sign of Pisces. "We can see from the example of Leviathan," he says, "how the great 'fish' gradually split into its opposite, after having itself been the opposite of the highest God and hence his shadow, the embodiment of his evil side."[22] One fish in Pisces is Leviathan (Antichrist), the shadow of the other fish, Ichthys (Christ). True to form, Moby

Dick, the White Whale, rises with Pisces on the first day of the chase and casts a "white shadow" on the surface of the sea (p. 447). The split in Moby Dick between substance and shadow is perfectly analogous to the split in Pisces between Ichthys and Leviathan, Christ and Antichrist, and to the split in Ahab's personality between good and evil, God and devil. The second mate says that "with Pisces, or the Fishes, we sleep" (p. 361). Ahab's propensity for projection is such that he does indeed sleep with Pisces, or Moby Dick—and the sleep he sleeps is the sleep of death.

Melville explicitly defines Ahab's psychological state as a monomaniac fixation, an irrational obsession with one subject only—in this case, with Moby Dick. But Melville also says that madness defies exact definition. As he puts it in *Billy Budd:*

> Who in the rainbow can draw the line where the violet tint ends and the orange tint begins? Distinctly we see the difference of the colors, but where exactly does the one first blendingly enter into the other? So with sanity and insanity. In pronounced cases there is no question about them. But in some supposed cases, in various degrees supposedly less pronounced, to draw the exact line of demarcation few will undertake, though for a fee becoming considerate some professional experts will. There is nothing namable but that some men will, or undertake to, do it for pay.[23]

Freudians and Jungians do undertake to draw the fine line, and they are well paid for their keen insight. But for Melville, sanity and insanity are relative terms, indefinable in all but the most conspicuous cases. Insanity and sanity (in Melville's words, "madness" and "right reason") are extremes of one, and their mutual extremism makes it difficult if not impossible to distinguish the abnormal from the normal. For example, Ahab knows that "all my means are sane, my motive and my object mad" (p. 161). At one extreme of his personality he is perfectly rational; at the other, he is absolutely irrational.

Melville employs the term "right reason" in *Mardi* as a synonym for the love of "Alma," or Christ: "Right-reason, and Alma, are the same; else Alma, not reason, would we reject. The Master's great command is Love; and here do all things wise, and all things good, unite. Love is all in all. The more we love, the more we know, and so reversed."[24] If madness and right reason are extremes of one, as Melville says, and if right reason is equivalent to love, then madness is equivalent to hate.

Madness and right reason are contraries of one paradoxical personality; they only become contradictories when that personality is split in two, as it is in Ahab's case. The oppositions good and evil, God and devil, substance and shadow, Ichthys and Leviathan, Christ and Antichrist, right reason and madness, love and hate, are interchangeable categories in Ahab's Jonah-and-the-Whale complex.

So also is the opposition white magic (Theurgic) and black magic (Goetic). Charles Olson employs a grammatical criterion in an effort to delimit the meaning of Melville's secret motto. He maintains that the phrase "not the (black art) Goetic but Theurgic magic" is a parenthetic expression, an appositive of the "one" of which madness and right reason are extremes—that is, of the one way to seek, as Melville says, "converse with the Intelligence, Power, the Angel," or, as Olson says, "quite simply, God." According to Olson, "'Goetic' might seem to derive from Goethe and thus *Faust*, but its source is the Greek 'goetos,'" which means magician. (Of course, "Goetic" may be, by means of false etymology, a deliberate pun on "goetos" and "Goethe," for Faust is a magician.) "Wherever Melville picked up the word, he means it, as he says, for the 'black art,'" the opposite of Theurgic, or the white art. Curiously enough, Olson contends that "white or 'Theurgic' magic, like 'madness' and 'right reason,' seeks God, while the 'black art Goetic' invokes only the devil." In other words, he asserts that not only right reason but also *madness* invokes God. But Ahab is mad, and he does not seek God; he seeks only the devil. The only magic that Ahab practices is Goetic. In this respect, Olson says that "Ahab's art, so long as his hate survives, is black. He does not seek true converse."[25] The blackness of Ahab's art is precisely the madness of it, the hate he projects onto the White Whale.

"Theurgic magic" is not, as Olson supposes, an appositive of "one"; it is simply the subject of the final sentence of Melville's secret motto. Otherwise, Melville has been ungrammatical indeed, for he has committed an elementary number error. In Olson's interpretation, the plural subject "It & right reason" disagrees with the singular verb "seeks." Madness and right reason may be extremes of one, but they are not, as Olson suggests, equally efficacious means to an end—which is true converse. Theurgic magic, right reason, or love seeks God; Goetic magic, madness, or hate seeks only the devil. Insofar as

Ahab is possessed by the devil—that is, by the demon or shadow archetype—he is utterly alienated from God. He is the madman as antihero, not merely demented but bedeviled and damned.

Notes

1. The present article (a version of which was presented at the Mid-Hudson Modern Language Association of America conference in November 1982) is a sequel to Michael Vannoy Adams, "Ahab's Jonah-and-the-Whale Complex: The Fish Archetype in *Moby-Dick,*" *Emerson Society Quarterly* 28, no. 3 (1982): 167–82. See also Adams, "Getting a Kick out of Captain Ahab: The Merman Dream in *Moby-Dick,*" *Dreamworks* 4, no. 4 (1984/85): 279–87, and "Whaling and Difference: *Moby-Dick* Deconstructed," *New Orleans Review* 10, no. 4 (Winter 1983): 59–64. The vast majority of contemporary literary critics exhibit no knowledge of the most recent trends in Jungian theory. (This is especially true of Freudian critics, who, consciously or unconsciously, perpetuate the personality cult of Freud and who maintain a conspiracy of silence in regard to Jung, but it is also true of Jungian critics.) Many critics are suspicious (or even contemptuous) of Jungian theory. What they do not yet realize is that there has been a radical revision of Jungian theory, away from interpretation (or conceptualization of the unconscious) and toward imagination. The most prominent exponent of this "re-visioning" of Jungian theory is James Hillman. In effect, what Hillman proposes is a "deconstruction" of traditional Jungian (and Freudian) methods. In this regard, see Adams, "Deconstructive Philosophy and Imaginal Psychology: Comparative Perspectives on Jacques Derrida and James Hillman," *Journal of Literary Criticism* 2, no. 1 (June 1985): 23–39. (This article was published at Allahabad University in India; copies of it may be obtained most easily directly from the author.) See also Paul Kugler, "Involuntary Poetics," *New Literary History* 15 (1983/84): 491–501; this article is a revision of the final chapter in Kugler, *The Alchemy of Discourse: An Archetypal Approach to Language* (Lewisburg, Penna: Bucknell University Press, 1982).

2. See John Halverson, "The Shadow in *Moby-Dick,*" *American Quarterly* 15 (1963): 436–46. Halverson was the first to attempt to demonstrate in a systematic way the relevance of Jung's archetype for Melville's novel.

3. Herman Melville, *Moby-Dick,* ed. Harrison Hayford and Hershel Parker (New York: Norton, 1967), p. 91; hereafter cited parenthetically in the text.

4. C. G. Jung, *Aion, The Collected Works,* 2d ed. (Princeton: Princeton University Press, 1968–83), 9 (pt. 2):30.

5. Jung, "On the Psychology of the Unconscious," *Works* 7:96–97.

6. Ibid., p. 96.

7. Jung, *Aion,* p. 8.

8. Jung, "Symbols and the Interpretation of Dreams," *Works* 18:210.

9. Jung, *Aion,* p. 8.

10. Ibid., p. 9.

11. Ibid.

12 Jung, "Appendix II: The Structure of the Unconscious," *Works* 7:274–75.

13. Melville to Nathaniel Hawthorne, 29 June 1851, *The Letters of Herman Melville,* ed. Merrell R. Davis and William H. Gilman (New Haven: Yale University Press, 1960), p. 133.

14. Melville to Nathaniel Hawthorne, 17 (?) November 1851, ibid., p. 142.

15. Quoted in Charles Olson, *Call Me Ishmael* (San Francisco: City Lights, 1947), p. 52.

16. Jung, "Psychology and Religion," *Works* 11:59.

17. Jung, "A Psychological Approach to the Trinity," *Works* 11:168. Cf. Victor White, *Soul and Psyche: An Inquiry into the Relationship of Psychotherapy and Religion* (New York: Harper and Brothers, 1960), pp. 95–114, 141–65.

18. "The Divinity School Address," *The Collected Works of Ralph Waldo Emerson*, ed. Alfred R. Ferguson et al. (Cambridge: Harvard University Press, 1971), 1:78.

19. Jung, *Aion*, p. 53.

20. Jung, *Answer to Job, Works* 11:357.

21. Jung, "Synchronicity: An Acausal Connecting Principle," *Works* 8:426.

22. Jung, *Aion*, p. 119.

23. Herman Melville, *Billy Budd: Sailor (An Inside Narrative)*, ed. Harrison Hayford and Merton M. Sealts, Jr. (Chicago: University of Chicago Press, 1962), p. 102.

24. Herman Melville, *Mardi and a Voyage Hither, The Writings of Herman Melville*, ed. Harrison Hayford, Hershel Parker, and G. Thomas Tanselle (Evanston, Ill.: Northwestern University Press, 1970), 3:629.

25. Olson, *Call Me Ishmael*, pp. 55–56.

Wallace Stevens's Pythoness

Barbara M. Fisher

City College of CUNY

I F Stevens's "interior paramour" is a Jungian anima figure or a moth-eaten "muse," as a number of readers have supposed, why doesn't she conform to the models? Why does she display characteristics that are sharply at variance with both the contemporary and classical figures? Can Stevens's intensely personal "paramour" be defined as a "collective projection of the masculine unconscious," as Michel Benamou has defined her? And can one really believe with Benamou that "Jungian psychology accounts rather well for this voice" in Stevens's poetry?[1]

More generally, can one reduce Stevens's complex response to the feminine to "an image of the great earth mother which will appear in various forms throughout the work," as Edward Kessler has done?[2] Is Stevens's woman "not an ideal but the earth itself," as Kessler defines her, also from a Jungian perspective. And can Stevens's vision of the feminine, that Kessler rightly identifies with "summer" and "south," also be understood as simple "physical sensation," or "the part of the world that can be enjoyed without explanation or meaning"? Kessler believes with Benamou that Stevens is "drawing upon a general archetype from the 'collective unconscious'" and, interestingly, he finds Stevens's image of woman "ambiguous or contradictory where the poet evokes a composite figure rather than a single representative."[3] Thus Kessler refers to the "disturbing" invocation—"Sister and Mother and diviner love"—that opens "To the One of Fictive Music," and to the "troublesome opening" of "Le Monocle de Mon Oncle": "Mother of Heaven, regina of the clouds, / O sceptre of the sun, crown of the moon." In truth, it is an extremely troublesome opening, particularly if one is compelled to interpret "heaven," "clouds," "sun" and "moon" as "the great earth mother" or as mindless physical sensation. Kessler cannot account for the striding poet-singer in "The Idea of Order at Key West" just as Jungian psychology cannot account for such a figure of the feminine within its limitations. Kessler sidesteps the difficulty by comparing Stevens's genius of the shore to Yeats's figure of "A Crazed Girl."[4]

The classical invocation to the "goddess" (Homer) or to the "divine muses" (Hesiod) was carried forward in English poetry as the invocation to Urania, the "heavenly muse." A. Walton Litz refers to this tradition when he calls the One of Fictive Music a "muse-goddess." The poem opens, says Litz, "with an invocation to the naked imagination, pure and simple, a figure of Muse and Virgin and earthly woman who is mistress of the music celebrated in the second stanza."[5] As Harold Bloom points out, Litz relates "Fictive Music" to the term *musica ficta* used by medieval theorists to describe "accidentals that lie outside of a harmonic system." Indeed, Litz's "mistress of music" rather transforms Stevens's figure into a latter-day Saint Cecelia of sorts, while the poem might be understood as a species of Birthday Ode to the patron saint of harmony and counterpoint. But if the One invoked is music's mistress, is it only Saint Cecelia or a Greek muse or pure "imagination" that will fit her description? Perhaps the "musician" of this early poem can also be traced to Stevens's beautiful wife, who gave music lessons as a young woman, and whose long golden hair has been memorialized in Stevens's poetry.[6] Be that as it may, "To the One of Fictive Music" certainly contains a partly amused nod to the Heliconian muses, and a more serious reflection on poetic musing—much like the double melody "Peter Quince" plays on the clavier, that plays in turn upon Peter Quince.

Bloom escorts the muse into Freudian territory. The One of Fictive Music is a "familial muse" according to Bloom. "Stevens takes the Oedipal risk, as Keats and Whitman did, and invokes the muse as his actual mother and as the other women of his family."[7] Bloom also uses "muse" interchangeably with "paramour" in his discussion of "Final Soliloquy of the Interior Paramour," the beautifully wrought chamberpiece of the very late poetry. Bloom declares, however, that the demonic circus freak, Madame La Fleurie—"a bearded queen, wicked in her dead light"[8]—is "the last version of the American muse-as-mother, and so a more authentic vision of the interior paramour."[9]

Litz's reading is always lucid and married to the text, while Bloom's essential understanding of Stevens as a Romantic confers a lyrical muse with rosy cheeks hovering over him as well as

the deadliest muse-as-mother-earth. But Stevens's "interior paramour" is neither dread mother nor classical muse nor merely
"imagination, pure and simple." The literary muse is con-
ventionally summoned from above and beyond—from her
perch on Mount Helicon. She represents inspiration that strikes
from without; she is external to the poet, alien, a "divine other."
The "paramour," in contrast, is an internal component, always
present within the poet's range of consciousness. She dwells in
"the hermitage at the centre"; she is the "sibyl of the self," an
interior love-object as against an exteriorized force. Bloom
comes closest to the *emotional* tension that obtains between poet
and paramour by way of his Freudian approach. Finally, the
classical muse speaks *to* the poet or *through* the poet: "Fool," says
Sidney's muse to him, "look in thy heart and write." Stevens
speaks *with* his paramour. In one sense, Stevens's paramour *is*
the knowledge of the heart, while their discourse is almost
always an interchange, "those exchanges of speech in which
your words are mine, mine yours."[10] Only once, in "Final Soliloquy," does the paramour speak with her own voice, and then
she is speaking for both. One is brought back, then, to the idea
of Stevens's paramour as anima or soul. But is it the anima
defined by Carl Jung, or does Stevens's interior presence depart
from Jungian notions of anima and animus? A close look at
Jung's description of the anima can be revealing, and I should
like to explore this Jungian archetype after a survey of Stevens's
references to the inner presence.

Although Stevens does not give the figure a name and, indeed, occasionally refers to it as "nameless," he invests his
"paramour" with a range of epithets and descriptive terms that
indicate a compound nature. Perhaps the essential fact about
the paramour is that the poet defines her as a "separate self."
The early "Re-statement of Romance" sets forth this relation
between poet and paramour:

> . . . Only we two may interchange
> Each in the other what each has to give.
> Only we two are one, not you and the night,
>
> Nor night and I, but you and I, alone
> So much alone, so deeply by ourselves,
> So far beyond the casual solitudes,

That night is only the background of our selves,
Supremely true each to its separate self,
In the pale light that each upon the other throws.

[*CP*, p. 146]

As one considers the manifestations of this separate self in the poetry it becomes increasingly clear that, like Theodore Roethke's flexible inamorata, Stevens's interior paramour has "more sides than a seal." She is portrayed with various colors and degrees of radiance ranging from "pale light" to flaming brilliance and, as Kessler and others have shown, she is related to summer and the south. Stevens's paramour has a dark and enigmatic side as well as a bright; far from Madame La Fleurie's bearded wickedness, however, she recalls the "black but comely" Shulamite of Solomon's love song. Indeed, her attributes point to two main sources beyond the Romantics: the Bernardine soul as *sponsa*, derived from the Song of Songs, and Plato's *Diotima*. Like the Soul of the Universe described in Plato's *Timaeus*, she is composed of "the same and of the other and of the essence."[11]

Stevens's paramour is the oracular "woman with the hair of a pythoness" (*NA*, p. 29) who is his internal "reader." Like Ariadne, she is the "inexplicable sister of the minotaur" who is herself "half beast and somehow more than human" (*NA*, p. 52). She is Memory in *Owl's Clover*, the essential recollection that is "mother of us all, / The earthly mother and the mother of / The dead" (*CP*, p. 432). She is the *noeud vital*, the "green queen" with the "green mind" (*CP*, p. 339) and the "abstract, the archaic queen" who "walks among astronomers" (*CP*, p. 223). She is Eve who "made air the mirror of herself" (*CP*, p. 383), and "the naked, nameless dame" whose hand "wove round her glittering hair" (*CP*, p. 271). She is "Fat girl, terrestrial, my summer, my night" (*CP*, p. 406), and "Donna, donna, dark / Stooping in indigo gown / And cloudy constellations" (*CP*, p. 48). Stevens invokes her with bitter irony and immense longing as "Mother of heaven, regina of the clouds" (*CP*, p. 13), but later she becomes the serene being "that was mistress of the world" (*CP*, p. 460) and the genetrix from whom all motion and existence proceeds: "Moving and being, the image at its source" (*CP*, p. 223). Like Shelley's *epipsyche*, she is "A Golden Woman in a Silver

Mirror" (*CP*, p. 460); like Plato's Diotima, she is the "sibyl of the self";[12] like Saint Bernard's *sponsa*, she is "the spouse, the bride" (*CP*, p. 396), "the desired . . . sleek in a natural nakedness" who lives in "The Hermitage at the Centre" (*CP*, p. 505). Like Blake's Divine Human Imagination, she is "the maker of the song" (*CP*, p. 129), and this is the one time—in "The Idea of Order at Key West"—that the paramour is projected as an exterior being. Finally, she is the curiously tripartite "One" of Fictive Music (*CP*, p. 87); the separate self "that speaks, denouncing separate selves" (*CP*, p. 441); the ambiguous "lover that lies within us" (*CP*, p. 394).

Stevens is sparing of the term "paramour." It occurs only four times in the complete poetry, and just once as "interior paramour." However, it is this single appearance in the title of a very late work that leads one to suspect that Stevens is using it as a generic term; he is allowing the reader a glimpse, at this late date, of a very private element of poetry. As the above catalogue indicates, Stevens's paramour is erotic, noetic, active, internal, and female. She is both earthy and celestial, dark and bright, covert and central. While transformations preserve the mystery that surrounds the paramour, her presence pervades the poetry and her aspects extend into the metaphysical, the mythic, and the oracular. She is, in essence, the creative anima of a poet who was roughly contemporary with Jung. How, then, does Stevens's richly articulated imagery of the paramour compare with Jung's archetypal concept of the anima?

The anima, according to Jung, is the image of the feminine that exists in the masculine psyche. It is a "projection" of the "mother imago" that extends into the image of "the daughter, the sister, the beloved, the heavenly goddess, and the earth spirit Baubo."[13] In his exposition of the anima in *Aion*, Jung stresses the universality of the "projection" which he discusses as though it were a disease:

> Every mother and every beloved is forced to become the carrier and embodiment of this omnipresent and ageless image which corresponds to the deepest reality in a man. It is his own, this perilous image of Woman.[14]

This "perilous image," says Jung, "stands for loyalty; she is the vital compensation . . . the solace . . . the great illusionist, the seductress."[15]

The equivalent archetype in the feminine psyche, according to this theory, is the animus or image of the father. Jung invests the masculine "imago" with the quality of "reason or spirit." Woman is "compensated by this masculine element," as Jung believes, and he goes on in his discussion of anima and animus to reduce the qualities that distinguish the masculine and the feminine into two opposed "projections": these are masculine rationality and feminine sensuality: "The animus corresponds to the paternal Logos just as the anima corresponds to the maternal Eros."[16]

One cannot fail to be impressed by the tidiness of this scheme. In "Marriage as a Psychological Relationship," Jung explains that "Woman has no anima, no soul, but she has an animus," but now he reiterates his theory with a slight twist: "the anima has an erotic, emotional character, the animus a rationalizing one."[17] The same element that is manifest in the "paternal Logos" as "rationality" becomes "rationalizing" when actually internalized by the daughter. Finally, in *Aion* Jung contradicts his former explanation of the anima as a "projection" of the masculine psyche. With no explanation, the character of the anima suddenly becomes the "true nature" of woman:

> I use Eros and Logos merely as conceptual aids to describe the fact that woman's consciousness is characterized more by the connective quality of Eros than by the discrimination and cognition associated with Logos. In men, Eros . . . is usually less developed than Logos. In women, on the other hand, Eros is an expression of their true nature, while their Logos is often only a regrettable accident.[18]

This rigid division of attributes that Jungian psychology honors as an archetype and which Jung himself sets forth as a universal truth, can hardly be said to "account rather well" for Stevens's complex paramour. The paramour is indeed an erotic presence, as noted above, but she also contains those qualities of "reason or spirit" that Jung assigns to the "masculine imago." Thus, Jungian psychology cannot comprehend a Stevensian paramour who is not only a love-object, intuitive, and emotional, but whose nature includes the inventive, the spiritual, the cognitive, and the discriminating. Stevens's interior paramour is, perhaps, like Psyche of the legend who bears a lighted candle through the night in her approach to (a very masculine) Eros: she dwells in darkness, yet illuminates the dark.

The anima is painted in its most Freudian colors in *Esthétique du Mal*, canto 10. Here Stevens, with sympathy and tact, identifies Beaudelaire's feeling for women as manifest in *Les Fleurs du Mal*:

> He sought the most grossly maternal, the creature
> Who most fecundly assuaged him, the softest
> Woman with a vague moustache and not the mauve
> *Maman*. His anima liked its animal
> And liked it unsubjugated, . . .

Stevens is clearly taking "the Oedipal risk" in this passage, as Bloom would say. But even if we take this to be a self-descriptive, rather than purely biographical, portrayal of desire and the artist, the anima figuration is vivid, energetic, manifold, while the passage itself is loaded with double entendres:

> so that home
> Was a return to birth, a being born
> Again in the savagest severity,
> Desiring fiercely, the child of a mother fierce
> In his body, fiercer in his mind, merciless
> To accomplish the truth in his intelligence.
> It is true there were other mothers, singular
> In form, lovers of heaven and earth, she-wolves
> And forest tigresses and women mixed
> With the sea. These were fantastic.

> [*CP*, p. 321]

It is not really helpful, I think, to define even this exaggerated figuration in terms of disease, or to discuss Stevens's paramour as a mental or emotional aberration, a "schizoid self," as Mary Arensberg does in "Wallace Stevens' Interior Paramour."[19] Nor does it add to one's understanding of Stevens's poetics to think of his paramour as a mere "syntactic event" (Arensberg here refers to Michael Beehler's critical approach), or to consider the paramour "an illusion, constructed within a linguistic hall of mirrors."[20] Nor can we think of the paramour as "an invented fiction . . . generated from within the poet's own psyche," if we recognize her both as a "separate self" and an integral part of the poet—possibly the very psyche that is said to be "generating" an "invented fiction" of itself.

In her reading of Stevens's "Final Soliloquy of the Interior

Paramour," Arensberg draws upon J. Hillis Miller's well-known essay, "Stevens' 'Rock' and Criticism as Cure," which leads her to apply therapeutic principles of psychodrama to a theory of the paramour. Arensberg seems content to present Miller's idea of "a shadowy psychodrama involving the difference of the sexes" as the foundation for a reading of "Final Soliloquy."[21] I do not want to dwell upon this "psychological" interpretation of Stevens's poem, but generally to stress that—as with Bloom's revisionist theory—one finds here an interpretation based on the influence of "anxiety," i.e., on a philosophy of the emotional imbalance of an age that blurs into a clinical area of mental disorder. Such readings often lack fine tuning. More important, they tend to conclusions in which quasi-medical "diagnoses" are dangerously presented as literary criticism. These "clinical" readings are inevitable in a school of criticism that treats poetry as a symptom of disease, and which relies heavily on borrowed terms of "repression" and "sublimation" to express controlled invention and creative figuration. Certainly, a "clinical" reading cannot begin to address the metaphysical or spiritual qualities inherent in Stevens's paramour. But, if Stevens's interior paramour is not a "schizoid self," or a Jungian construct of the "mother imago," or yet a traditional "muse" who strikes from above, to what—in the rabbis' ancient formula—can she be compared?

The idea of a "cognitive" component in the anima goes back to the classical tradition of *Nous* (or *Noys*), a philosophic conceptualization of the intellective soul. Stevens's interior paramour—as we learn in "Re-statement of Romance"—is not only the "other," but also "together with" and "part of" the one who speaks with her. As noted earlier, she shares these attributes with Plato's Soul of the Universe, described in the passage on the Creation in the *Timaeus*. Plato describes the composition of the soul, here, her motion, and her intellective functions. These last, interestingly enough, are the ability to discriminate, which Jung assigns to the "paternal Logos," and the ability to define relationships, which Jung accords to the "maternal Eros." The Soul, says Plato,

> is composed of the same and of the other and of the essence, these three, and is divided and united in due proportion, and in her revolutions returns upon herself. The soul, when touching anything which has essence . . . is stirred through all her powers to

declare the sameness or the difference of that thing and some other; and to what individuals are related, and by what affected, and in what way and how and when.[22]

Plato tells us that although "the soul is invisible," she "partakes of reason and harmony." Stevens carries this concept of mind into the figure of the "green queen" in "Description Without Place": "Her green mind made the world around her green" (*CP*, p. 339). In the earlier "The Candle of a Saint," this archaic concept of mind is reflected in "she that walks among astronomers . . . like a noble figure out of the sky." Again lit by and dressed in green—"green kindled and apparelled"—she is

> The noble figure, the essential shadow,
>
> Moving and being, the image at its source,
> The abstract, the archaic queen.

> [*CP*, p. 223]

Stevens's figure of "the abstract, the archaic queen" as the embodiment of a noetic principle has its antecedents in Western thought. To find the intellective principle in female form, however, one must travel back by way of Christian Platonism to the *Noys* of Bernard Silvestris in the twelfth century, and further back to the *Nous* of Plotinus in the third, taking note of Plotinus' account of the nature of *Aphrodite Ouranos*. Moving into classical times, one notes the role of Plato's Diotima in the *Symposium* and her continuity with a presocratic intellective principle embodied by Parmenides' Goddess in *The Way of Truth*. Perhaps the divine *Tetractys* that formed the core of Pythagorean mystical mathematics feeds into this tradition.

Before turning to Diotima, Socrates' oracular priestess and "instructress in the ways of love . . . and many other things," I should like to briefly note the characteristics of the noetic principle in the Christian era. George Economou has summarized the nature of Bernard Silvestris's *Noys* from her opening remarks in *De universitate mundi* (*On the Universe*):

Generated by God, she is his eternal and divine reason; she is not in time. In her are situated the eternal ideas and the intelligible world; the destiny of all God's creatures is mirrored in her. Because she is the intellect of the supreme God, born of his divinity, she cannot be separated from the nature and substance of God.[23]

Silvestris's *Noys* (from Greek *nous*, or mind) is "divine reason," the "intellect of the supreme God." In a way, she resembles the Hebrew *Shekina* who is said to be the "radiance" of God. Plotinus is closer to the pagan tradition. In his discussion of *Aphrodite Ouranos* in the third *Ennead*, the intellectual principle is seen, not as an attribute of God, but *as* God:

> The Heavenly Aphrodite . . . who is none other than the Intellectual Principle—must be the soul at its divinest: unmingled . . . remaining forever Above, never having developed the downward tendency . . . a Divine Hypostasis essentially aloof . . . mythically the "unmothered"—justly called not Celestial Spirit but God.[24]

One finds this "archaic" idea of the intellectual principle in Stevens's poetry, manifesting itself in various representations of the interior paramour—and in this as much as in anythng, Stevens swerves away from his contemporaries, notably Williams and Pound, and to a lesser extent, Yeats and Eliot. In "The Figure of the Youth as Virile Poet," Stevens defines "our nature" as a "limitless space through which the intelligence moves without coming to an end" (*NA*, p. 53). This "intelligence," he observes, has replaced the Miltonic muse in our time. Our era has produced "a muse of its own, still half-beast and somehow more than human" that accompanies the developing poet and embodies the intelligence that endures. This half-beastly Ariadne provides a clue to the nature of Stevens's paramour. At the conclusion of the essay, Stevens invokes the enigmatic muse-*cum*-beast in Yeatsian terms:

> Inexplicable sister of the Minotaur, enigma and mask, although I am part of what is real, hear me and recognize me as part of the unreal. I am the truth, but the truth of the imagination of life in which with unfamiliar motion and manner you guide me in those exchanges of speech in which your words are mine, mine yours. [*NA*, p. 67]

It is remarkable how many elements are compressed into this statement. There is the rapt quality of the invocation, the mythic echoes and the oracular edge to it; the idea of the strangely beautiful and grotesquely frightening; the "unfamiliar" and "unreal" that is situated within the familiar and the "real." There is the barbaric, half-monstrous archaic image, and the interdialogic exchange in which poet and inner voice mingle enough to speak out as a single voice. Yet, dense as this sister-of-the-Minotaur passage is, all of the elements in it are further compressed into a single stunning image in "The Noble Rider and the Sound of Words." In this essay, which opens with the winged horses and charioteer of the *Phaedrus*, we are almost casually introduced to Stevens's version of Plato's mantic priestess: "All poets address themselves to someone," says Stevens, "and it is of the essence of that instinct . . . that it should be to an elite, not to a drab but to a woman with the hair of a pythoness" (*NA*, p. 29).

"A woman with the hair of a pythoness" is not, as one may first imagine, a Medusa with hair composed of wildly twining snakes. Once summoned up, however, the Medusa image does not dissipate entirely; it remains long enough to ensure the barbarity of the pythoness image, to intensify its uncanny quality, and to sharpen its archaic outline. The pythoness is a sibyl, of course, the oracular priestess who presided in ancient times at Delphi. When Apollo replaced the original deity at the serpent's shrine, the pythoness continued as the voice of the Delphic oracle—that same oracle consulted in legend by Oedipus and in history by Socrates himself. Plato tells us that his teacher returned from this encounter with an additional inner voice that he referred to as his demon. In the *Symposium*, Plato combines the guiding voice of Socrates' demon and the priestess of the oracle in the character of Diotima the Mantinaean. And throughout the dialogues, one finds no more "elite" or more "interior" personage than she.

The relation of poetry to philosophy was a question that fascinated Stevens, who returned to it again and again. What he came to was that all creative thought is poetic, i. e., the result of poiesis. "Philosophers . . . are not limited to reason," he observes in "A Collect of Philosophy," "their ideas are often a triumph of the imagination" (*OP*, p. 200). More than any other Platonic dialogue, the *Symposium* deals with the relation of poetry to philosophy, and with the contrasts involved in their pursuit. It is significant in this context that Diotima's exposition on the true nature of love, which constitutes the heart of the *Symposium*, employs both literary forms and philosophic reasoning. It begins with Socratic questioning, progresses through a parodic allegorical fable, pauses to define poiesis in ontological terms—"All creation or passage of non-being into being is poetry or making"[25]—develops epistemological concepts that parallel the theory of the "divided line" in the *Republic*, and concludes with the closest thing to a rhapsodic flight that one finds outside the *Phaedrus*.

Diotima's discourse is in reality Socrates' speech; Plato has her "stand in" for the elder philosopher. It is the relationship between these two figures that contributes to an understanding of Stevens's paramour and suggests in what respects the character of Diotima serves as source and model for Stevens's interior "other." In the *Symposium*, Socrates introduces Diotima (whose name invokes ideas of divinity and honor, from *dio* and *tima*) during an exchange with the poet Agathon, recalling to memory the "instructress" of his youth whom he describes as "a woman wise in love and in many other kinds of knowledge."[26] Within this frame, Diotima begins her discourse precisely where Socrates leaves off and in the same dialectical mode. Now, however, Socrates is the young and ignorant responder and his instructress the wise questioner. That a dialectical exchange takes place in a Platonic dialogue is no cause for surprise. What is unusual about the *Symposium* is that virtually the whole of Socrates' discussion of the *true* nature of love is presented as the teaching of an oracular voice out of the past, and in terms of a *recollection*.

I should like to underscore the significance of "recollection" (anamnesis) or true memory in Plato's theory of knowledge. F. M. Cornford puts it concisely that "all learning is the recovery of latent knowledge always possessed by the immortal soul."[27] If this principle is applied to the characters in the *Symposium*, it suggests that the wisdom Socrates says he has derived from Diotima is actually the recovery of knowledge always possessed by his own soul. It seems that Plato is indicating an even closer relation between Socrates and the prophetess than that of student and teacher in the art of love. Although she is introduced as a living woman with a history and location, on some level Diotima is meant to be understood as the prophetic and knowing component of Socrates' nature: his immortal soul. Diotima, to use Stevens's phrase, is Socrates' "sibyl of the self."

Beside the pagan intellective principle and the platonic notion of the soul, Stevens's interior paramour reflects a later concept of the soul as bride or *sponsa*. This mystical erotic concept of the soul, drawn from the Song of Songs and developed in Christian speculative theology, attaches to the "burning body" of Stevens's "contemplated spouse" in "Notes toward a Supreme Fiction" (*CP*, p. 395) and to "the desired" who is "sleek in a natural nakedness" in "The Hermitage at the Centre" (*CP*, p. 505). The lyric sensuality of Canticles invests these lines:

> How soft the grass on which the desired
> Reclines in the temperature of heaven—

In "The Hand as a Being," the allusion to Canticles is explicit while the "knowing" that develops between the poet and the woman, whose hand "wove round her glittering hair," has a clear biblical sense:

> In the first canto of the final canticle.
> Her hand took his and drew him near to her.
> Her hair fell on him and the mi-bird flew
>
> To the ruddier bushes at the garden's end.
> Of her, of her alone, he knew
> And lay beside her underneath the tree.

> [*CP*, p. 271]

This mediating "she" and the act of loving union parallels the union of the soul with the Word as expounded by Origen, by the Areopagite, by the Victorines, and with great lucidity by Saint Bernard. Bernard writes of the mystical hierogamy of human soul and divine Logos in a deeply personal way. One sees mirrored in the passage below the psychological space, the "irrational" mode of intuitive knowledge, and the bridal sensuousness of Stevens's paramour:

> A soul thus loving and thus loved will not be satisfied . . . with that manifestation of the bridegroom which is made to few through visions and dreams, unless . . . it may also receive him in the very marrow of its heart, and may have its beloved in its presence, not perceived but absorbed, not appearing but affecting; and no doubt the more delightful for being inward, not outward.[28]

When we turn to "Final Soliloquy of the Interior Paramour," we will find these Bernardine qualities once more in a presence "the more delightful for being inward," in a beloved who is "not perceived but absorbed, not appearing but affecting." However, if one returns to the Song of Songs itself, and to the passionate Shulamite who searches and longs for her beloved, the theological mystique clears off and one is brought back to the headiness of purely physical pleasures: "Let him kiss me with the kisses of his mouth: for your love is better than wine." The Shulamite, who provides the model for the soul in love, calls her bridegroom a "dove that art in the clefts of the rock," a "young hart upon the mountains," and "an apple tree among trees of the wood." She in turn is a "garden inclosed . . . my sister, my spouse"; she is "fair as the moon, clear as the sun," and, importantly, "black but comely." Thus, the Shulamite is a particularly rich source for Stevens's "beloved," for both her shining aspects and her dark face are mirrored in the paramour.

The shining aspect is uppermost in "To the One of Fictive Music," who is also sister and spouse, of sorts, and a creature of "flame and summer and sweet fire." Note the radiance Stevens casts about his tripartite One:

> Sister and mother and diviner love,
> And of the sisterhood of the living dead
> Most near, most clear, and of the clearest bloom,
> And of the fragrant mothers the most dear
> And queen, and of diviner love the day
> And flame and summer and sweet fire, no thread
> Of cloudy silver sprinkles in your gown
> Its venom of renown, and on your head
> No crown is simpler than the simple hair.

[*CP*, p. 87]

While her triple character of sister, mother, and divine beloved relates Stevens's invoked One more to a preclassical goddess than to any particular muse, the term "diviner"—repeated twice in this stanza—also carries the sense of augury. It calls up the idea of clairvoyance along with heavenly Aphrodite as "diviner love." Surely, this "diviner love," with her oracular quality and "crown of simple hair" bears a resemblance to that other, uncanny "woman with the hair of a pythoness."

But Stevens's invocation raises the One of Fictive Music from among the "sisterhood of the living dead"—the clan Muse. Both a sublime figure and a poetic mode exhumed from the past are brought to half-life again in a faintly ironic present. In this, Stevens follows Blake who laments that the "antient" muses have forsaken Poetry and withdrawn into the elements of the natural world: "Wandering in many a coral grove, / Fair Nine, forsaking Poetry!"[29] The "celestial paramours" of *Owl's Clover* are similarly muse figures, and ironic echoes of a moribund sublime. Their "awkward steps" describe a *danse macabre* while the atmosphere is weighted with Beaudelairean correspondences, unmistakable in "holy caverns temple-toned," and the sickly pallor of "wax-like blooms":

> Come, all celestial paramours,
> Whether in-dwelling haughty clouds, frigid,
> And crisply musical, or holy caverns temple-toned
> Entwine your arms and moving to and fro,
> Now like a ballet infantine in awkward steps,
> Chant sibilant requiems for this effigy.
> Bring down from nowhere nothing's wax-like blooms,
> In a mortal lullaby, like porcelain.

[*OP*, p. 47]

But these "infantine" and somehow deadly paramours evolve into dancers full of vital movement—"Weaving ring in radiant ring"—and take on both the bright and dark aspects of the beloved. They are first clothed in shining darkness:

> As if your gowns were woven of the light
> Yet were not bright, came shining as things come
> That enter day from night, come mirror-dark,
> With each fold sweeping in a sweeping play.

[*OP*, p. 51]

In the end, they are swept up in the same sensual and metaphysical fires that surround the One of Fictive Music, transformed into frankly impassioned "seducers and seduced" like the lover and beloved of the Canticles. The paramours are now

> fair and bloomed,
> No longer of air but of the breathing earth,
> Impassioned seducers and seduced, the pale
> Pitched into swelling bodies, upward, drift
> In a storm blown into glittering shapes, and flames
> Wind-beaten into freshest, brightest fire.

[*OP*, p. 52]

Although both the dark and bright aspects of the paramour are related to summer and the south, the dark face is most often associated with the southern night. Black, for Stevens, is neither absence of color nor lack of light, but an erotic and enveloping ambiance that is rich with anticipation and limitless possibilities. In "Two Figures in Dense Violet Light," the lover can be heard to whisper:

> Be the voice of night and Florida in my ear.
> Use dusky words and dusky images.
> Darken your speech.

> [*CP*, p. 86]

Stevens both reveals and conceals the presence of the dark paramour in "Six Significant Landscapes":

> The night is of the color
> Of a woman's arm;
> Night, the female,
> Obscure,
> Fragrant and supple,
> Conceals herself.

Again, there is a shining quality within this darkness:

> A pool shines,
> Like a bracelet
> Shaken in a dance.

> [*CP*, p. 73]

The poet is a "scholar of darkness" in the early "O Florida, Venereal Soil," and his inamorata "lascivious as the wind." As in so many of Stevens's "Florida" poems, a terrain is projected into a psychological interior and shaped into a woman's image. Here, the "Venus-like" body of the beloved place and climate is "absorbed" (to use Saint Bernard's term) into the dark-aspected figure of the paramour. The southern night becomes a black, but comely personage:

> Donna, donna dark,
> Stooping in indigo gown
> And cloudy constellations,

Conceal yourself or disclose
Fewest things to the lover—

[*CP*, p. 48]

Both "faces" of Stevens's paramour are enclosed within the
term itself. *Paramour*—meaning the "illicit partner of a married
man or woman"—entered English from Old French *par amur*,
"with love," or "by (means of) love." This is the aspect of
Stevens's paramour that he associates with "sweet fire" and
surrounds with hues of rose and gold and radiant luminosity.
The dark face of the paramour turns on a homonymic value:
the final syllable can be heard as *–moor*. Partridge traces English
Moor (for a North African Arab) from the Old French *More*,
deriving ultimately from Greek *mauros*, meaning "very dark." It
is the "night" face of the beloved who conceals herself and
discloses "fewest things to the lover."

In Solomon's love song, the dusky Shulamite cries out to the
elements: "Awake, O north wind; and come, thou south: blow
upon my garden, that the spices thereof may flow out" (4:16).
The poet of "Farewell to Florida" seems to turn his back upon
such a call as this with a sublime pathos. The poem stands at the
beginning of *Ideas of Order* (1936), and some readers feel that
the passage from south to north in it symbolizes a change of
poetics, and that the crossover marks the closing of an era.
Surely a profound leave-taking is in process:

Go on, high ship, since now, upon the shore,
The snake has left its skin upon the floor.
Key West sank downward under massive clouds
And silvers and greens spread over the sea. The moon
Is at the mast-head and the past is dead.
Her mind will never speak to me again.
I am free.

[*CP*, p. 117]

Perhaps these grave, stately measures studded with internal
rhyme presage a movement from the high romantic to the high
ironic. Bloom finds the stanza that follows this opening an
extraordinarily sensuous evocation, not of a state of the union
but "a state of mind." It is "so erotic a stanza," says Bloom, "that
the reader needs to keep reminding himself that this Florida, as
a state of mind, is a trope of pathos, a synechdoche for desire

and not desire itself."[30] Yet in this stanza, desire twists into death. The Shulamite's north and south winds that fan and enflame desire become, in Stevens's poem, "My North of cold whistled in a sepulchral South." The stanza follows:

> Her mind had bound me round. The palms were hot
> As if I lived in ashen ground, as if
> The leaves in which the wind kept up its sound
> From my North of cold whistled in a sepulchral South,
> Her South of pine and coral and coraline sea,
> Her home, not mine, in the ever-freshened Keys,
> Her days, her oceanic nights, calling
> For music, for whisperings from the reefs.
> How content I shall be in the North to which I sail
> And to feel sure and to forget the bleaching sand.

> [*CP*, p. 117]

One feels the wrench of these lines; this is departure from a beloved who is still loved. The agon between North and South here is one between passion and reason, and the seduction *and* destruction of the place the poet is putting behind him is manifest in the Siren images of "calling / For music" and "whisperings from the reefs," and the "bleaching sand." The mania of eros and poiesis is rejected in favor of the sanity and "contentment" of ordinary existence. Contentment of course is not bliss, not even painful bliss. It is a difficult moment in the poetry, and a stern passage toward North and sanity, for as we find in the fourth and final stanza:

> My north is leafless and lies in a wintry slime
> Both of men and clouds, a slime of men and crowds.

> [CP, p. 118]

One may sail determinedly north and away from Florida, but can one leave an "interior paramour" behind? I am not going to discuss "The Idea of Order at Key West" here—the poem has been read with fine sensitivity by a number of critics, and from a variety of approaches. I would like to suggest, however, that there may well be a connection between the passion and finality of "Farewell to Florida," in which the poet quits the shores of Key West, watching it sink "downward under massive clouds," and the subsequent emergence of the singer of the shore in

"The Idea of Order at Key West." In the "Farewell," we hear that "the snake has left its skin upon the shore." In the "Idea of Order," there is the sudden, striking appearance of the paramour as an externalized presence—the one time in the poetry, to my knowledge, that the sibyline creative element within jumps out of her skin, so to speak, like a snake. She is "appearing" here, in Bernard's terms, rather than absorbed. The singer of Key West is the genius of presence, the constructor of the here and now. But she is even more penetratingly the genius loci, if one understands that the locus in this poem is not so much a "place" as a threshold—for the singer strides along the margins of sea and shore and sky. In "The Idea of Order at Key West," the "enigma and mask" is unmasked: "the sea was not a mask. No more was she" (*CP*, p. 128). But like Echo, the singer is "unmasked" as pure presence with a voice. We can hear her continuo over the pounding surf, but only the poet sees the striding figure and only he knows who the nameless "she" really is.

In "Farewell to Florida," the poet means to detach entirely from the dark paramour. He intends that "she will not follow" or be part of him, except as memory:

> To stand here on the deck in the dark and say
> Farewell and to know that the land is forever gone
> And that she will not follow in any word
> Or look, nor ever again in thought, except
> That I loved her once.

[*CP*, p. 118]

"To know that the land is forever gone" conveys the same sense of despairing relinquishment that invests the final lines of Dylan Thomas's "Fern Hill": "to wake to the farm forever fled from the childless land"—the fall out of innocence into bitter knowledge. Stevens does sail north to a wintry "slime of men and crowds," and, in the superbly controlled "Idea of Order at Key West," manages to thrust the paramour outside the self. This once, in the poetry, the sibyl is transferred to an exterior plane and she moves along the edges of the marginal world, haunting the dimly starred threshold of the possible. But she does not remain in permanent exile. Toward the end of the poetry when Stevens is in his seventies, we are given the "Final

Soliloquy of the Interior Paramour," and only then is it clear that she has been with him all along.

Although "Final Soliloquy of the Interior Paramour" is structured as a *theoria,* a meditative review of knowing and being, and although it involves both mystical and theological concepts of "poverty" and "ultimate good," it stands essentially as a love poem. But it is an elegy as well as an epithalamion, its tones both muted and ringing, for it is a meditation of some gravity spun on the threshold of death and a marriage hymn sung "in the evening air." "Final Soliloquy" is also a poem of praise, cast in the Stevensian vernacular. It opens on a note of promise, grows from subdued acceptance to a swelling exaltation, resolves in a chord of sufficiency and completion—rare in the canon—while the overtone of promise holds throughout the poem.

This poem concerns the "intensest rendezvous," an encounter between "separate selves" that has developed beyond the interchange of the earlier "Re-statement of Romance." The two entities have become resolved, finally, "into one thing / Within a single thing." Bloom calls "Final Soliloquy" the "last of the great poems of 1950," and suggests that the title implies "not that the muse is about to perish but that poet and muse are about to be joined so that every remaining poem will be a dialogue of one."[31] I would only qualify that "Final Soliloquy" already *is* a dialogue of one, that Bloom's "about to be joined" is a resolution already accomplished, for the poem is cast in the immediate present. Again, the voice in "Final Soliloquy" does not speak as "I" in a first-person singular, or in the apparent plural—"we two together side by side"—but in a much older expression of dual personhood, the "dual" of Greek love poetry: "we two together, thinking, feeling, knowing as one being." As the title indicates, it is the paramour's voice that we hear—perhaps for the first time—articulately speaking for both poet and paramour, perhaps *as* both:

> Light the first light of evening, as in a room
> In which we rest and, for small reason, think
> The world imagined is the ultimate good.
>
> This is, therefore, the intensest rendezvous.
> It is in that thought that we collect ourselves,
> Out of all the indifferences, into one thing:

> Within a single thing, a single shawl
> Wrapped tightly around us, since we are poor, a warmth,
> A light, a power, the miraculous influence.
>
> Here, now, we forget each other and ourselves.
> We feel the obscurity of an order, a whole,
> A knowledge, that which arranged the rendezvous.
>
> Within its vital boundary, in the mind.
> We say God and the imagination are one . . .
> How high that highest candle lights the dark.
>
> Out of this same light, out of the central mind,
> We make a dwelling in the evening air,
> In which being there together is enough.

$$[CP, \text{p. } 524]$$

Although the poet is subject to age and time, his paramour is not. As the inner being that has to do with imagination, invention, memory, and oracular or "more than rational" knowledge, she is a mediating element, the instrument by which one reaches past time, beyond mortality. She is, perhaps, the equivalent of that "instrumental" soul in Donne's penultimate hymn, that must be tuned at the door to the "Holy roome." Stevens's late poem has much the same tonal quality as Donne's:

> Since I am comming to that Holy roome,
>   Where, with thy Quire of Saints for evermore,
> I shall be made thy Musique; As I come
>   I tune the instrument here at the dore,
> And what I must doe then, thinke now before.[32]

"Final Soliloquy" is illuminated by an eros principle that manifests itself as love of "ourselves," as selfless love in "we forget each other and ourselves," and finally as "the miraculous influence." Stevens places this sublime form of love at the exact center of the poem. By means of the "miraculous influence," a single light grows to illumine the whole of darkness; "small reason" reaches out to touch a "central mind"; emotion, perception, intuition, and thought are joined: "we feel . . . a knowledge . . . in the mind." The "world imagined" is transformed into a "spiritual dwelling"; obscurity is exchanged for knowledge, "good" becomes God in man, and solitude becomes companionship.

In a way, the couple in "Final Soliloquy" are like an old

married pair, wrapped as they are in a common shawl of faith or familiarity, although the quietude and humility that pervade the poem recall the qualities of Bernardine theology. In speculative theology, too, one finds the elegiac mode merging with the epithalamic, for the moment of death is also the moment of sublime union between *sponsa* and *sponsus*. In "Final Soliloquy," the notion of yielding and surrender is contained in the twice-repeated term, "rendezvous." Beyond the sense of an appointed time and its meaning of a love tryst, Stevens is drawing upon the term's Old French military sense of "Rendez-vous": "Give yourselves up!" These themes of surrender and humility are deepened in effect by the admission of poverty. As in Bernard's monastic philosophy, it is only "since we are poor" and somehow become naked that the compound soul is able to receive "a warmth, a power, the miraculous influence."

The voice of the paramour speaks out for the poet, in "Final Soliloquy," for much the same reasons that Diotima speaks the discourse of Socrates in the *Symposium*. She personifies his divine intellective principle—his immortal soul—and expresses the driving desire of that principle. The paramour's discourse, like Diotima's, is an instruction in the art of love, and, like Diotima's oracular revelation, is a teaching that points to an ultimate union with "ultimate good." But the paramour's first words are a revelation in themselves. "Light the first light of evening" is an echo, not of Socratic reasoning or platonic forms, but of the first spoken words in Genesis: "And God said, Let there be light, and there was light."

"Final Soliloquy of the Interior Paramour" constructs a delicate monument in praise of love and consecrates the union of poet and pythoness. During this "intensest rendezvous," the voice of the paramour chants a *requiescat* in a room that, like Donne's "Holy roome," is at once the place of final rest, a marriage chamber, and a metaphysical dwelling irradiated by divine influence. It is a room where the erotic is at one with the sacramental, where poet and paramour are "collected . . . into one thing," where very simply "being there together is enough."

Notes

1. Michel Benamou, "Art, Music, Angels and Sex: A Note on the Shorter Poems of *The Auroras of Autumn*," Wallace Stevens Journal 2 (Spring 1978): 3–9.

2. Edward Kessler, *Images of Wallace Stevens* (New Brunswick, N.J.: Rutgers University Press, 1972), pp. 16–17.

3. Ibid., p. 22.

4. Ibid., pp. 100–101.

5. A. Walton Litz, *Introspective Voyager: The Poetic Development of Wallace Stevens* (New York: Oxford University Press, 1972), p. 118.

6. Also see Holly Stevens's reference to her mother's hair in "Holidays in Reality," *Wallace Stevens: A Celebration*, ed. Frank Doggett and Robert Buttel (Princeton: Princeton University Press, 1980), pp. 105–6.

7. Harold Bloom, *Wallace Stevens: The Poems of Our Climate* (Ithaca, N.Y.: Cornell University Press, 1977), pp. 45–46.

8. Wallace Stevens, *The Collected Poems of Wallace Stevens* (New York: Knopf, 1954), p. 507; hereafter *CP*, with page numbers cited in the text.

9. Bloom, *Wallace Stevens*, pp. 359–60.

10. Wallace Stevens, *The Necessary Angel: Essays on Reality and the Imagination* (New York: Knopf, 1951), p. 76; hereafter *NA*, with page numbers cited in the text.

11. Plato, *Timaeus*, *The Dialogues of Plato*, trans. Benjamin Jowett (New York: Random House, 1937), 2:18.

12. Wallace Stevens, *Opus Posthumous*, ed. Samuel French Morse (New York: Knopf, 1957), p. 104; hereafter *OP*, with page numbers cited in the text.

13. C. G. Jung, "The Syzygy: Anima and Animus," *Aion, The Collected Works*, 2d ed. (Princeton: Princeton University Press, 1968–83), 9 (pt. 2):12–13.

14. Ibid., p. 13.

15. Ibid.

16. Ibid., p. 14.

17. Jung, "Marriage as a Psychological Relationship," *Works* 17:198.

18. Jung, "The Syzygy," p. 14.

19. Mary Arensberg, "Wallace Stevens' Interior Paramour," *Wallace Stevens Journal* 3 (Spring 1979):3–7.

20. Ibid. The reference is to Michael Beehler's "Meteoric Poetry: Wallace Stevens' 'Description Without Place,'" *Criticism* 29 (1977):241–59.

21. Ibid. Arensberg's reference here is to J. Hillis Miller's "Stevens' 'Rock' and Criticism as Cure," *Georgia Review* 30 (1976):1–28.

22. Plato, *Timaeus*, p. 18.

23. George Economou, *The Goddess Natura in Medieval Literature* (Cambridge: Harvard University Press, 1972), p. 152. Also see E. R. Curtius, *European Literature and the Latin Middle Ages*, trans. Willard R. Trask (Princeton: Princeton University Press, 1953), pp. 108–11, and Theodore Silverstein, "The Fabulous Cosmogony of Bernardus Silvestris," *Modern Philology* 66 (1948):95–98.

24. Plotinus, *The Enneads*, trans. Stephan MacKenna (London: Faber & Faber, 1962), *Ennead* 3.5, p. 193.

25. Plato, *Symposium, Dialogues of Plato*, 1:330.

26. Ibid., p. 327.

27. F. M. Cornford, *Plato's Theaetetus* (Indianapolis, Ind.: Bobbs-Merrill, 1959), pp. 27–28.

28. G. B. Burch, *Early Medieval Philosophy* (New York: King Crown Press, 1951), p. 98.

29. William Blake, "To the Muses," *The Poetry and Prose of William Blake*, ed. David V. Erdman and Harold Bloom (Garden City, N. Y.: Doubleday, 1970), pp. 408–9.

30. Bloom, *Wallace Stevens*, pp. 110–11.

31. Ibid., p. 359.

32. John Donne, "Hymne to God my God, in my sicknesse," *Seventeenth-Century English Poetry*, ed. Miriam Starkman (New York: Knopf, 1967), 1:109.

Style and Structure in Stevens's

The Auroras of Autumn

Nancy Prothro Arbuthnot

U. S. Naval Academy

AT the same time that Stevens was writing the poems that would compose *The Auroras of Autumn*, he published an essay on John Crowe Ransom that tells us as much about Stevens's own concerns as it does about Ransom's. Speaking of the sense of place that comes across in Ransom's works, Stevens says:

> One turns with something like ferocity toward a land that one loves, to which one is really and essentially native, to demand that it surrender, reveal, that in itself which one loves. This is a vital affair, not an affair of the heart (as it may be in one's first poems), but an affair of the whole being (as in one's last poems) a fundamental affair of life, or rather, an affair of fundamental life; so that one's cry of O Jerusalem becomes little by little a cry to something a little nearer until at last one cries out to a living name, a living place, a living thing, and in crying out confesses openly all the bitter secretions of experience.[1]

This passage, deeply personal as it is, allows us to put the late poems of Stevens into autobiographical perspective. In *The Auroras of Autumn*, we are struck with the sense that Stevens looks on these as possibly his last poems. Almost more than any others, they strike us as affairs of the whole being, of the meditating heart and mind. They name the "living place" where Stevens grew up—the Schuylkill and Swatara Rivers, the old Lutheran bells of the churches of his Pennsylvania home. These poems begin as "a children's tale of ice" but become a "sheen of heat" as memory takes on its own warm life. Extended now into autobiographical significance, the familiar Stevens characters—rabbi, reader, writer as reader, archetypal female as earth principle, male as imagination—and familiar images— river, rock, threshold, seasonal change—take on the emotional coloring of self-reference. Resonating with the orphic voice of Yeats at the end of his life, the vatic voice of St. John the Divine, the poems announce and reveal the dissolution of the world. The voice of the rabbi, that large red man reading, echoing after the book is closed, is the voice of John, calling his people. But the majestic tone is muted by the sense of a personal ending, pierced by a despair, the "bitter secretions" of the experience of loss and of death. Stevens's cancelations are, however, never final, and after the last echoings of disaster have died down, we see that *Auroras* is not a single-toned volume after all, but plays in a variety of keys: of assertion, hesitation, nostalgia, fear, faith, in addition to the slightly bitter despair. But this bitterness and fear modulate, if not into the positive assertions of belief we see in his later poems in *The Rock* and *Opus Posthumous*, at least into the finer tones of loss. In contrast to the obscure but powerful last poems, the short poems in *Auroras* seem especially accessible with their focus on "normal life, insight into the commonplace, reconciliation with every-day reality"[2] and help broaden our conception of Stevens's emotional range. A study of the style and structure of these short poems, relatively neglected in Stevens studies,[3] will help us better appreciate the depth and broadness of Stevens's range.

The Auroras of Autumn is a work dominated at first by long poems and large landscapes: the ice theatres of the title poem, the endless elaborations of "An Ordinary Evening in New Haven."[4] Poems of intense, though also subdued, drama place small human figures—Hans and José, mother, father and chil-dren—against the immense, inhuman landscape of the frozen north. But the grandness of the poems is also placed on a human scale by the "blooded" quality of the symbols and the voice not only prophetic but also extremely personal. Further, the drama of the poems helps personalize them. Many of the poems present dramatic situations of characters facing death: Hans struggling to survive the cold beside a driftwood fire; José apprehensive about the fate of an Argentine writer, frozen to death in a Paris hotel; the mother's face warming the room where the children gather, but not lighting it enough to dim the blazing of the death-foreboding auroras outside. Such poems portray characters interacting—or failing to interact—with the world and with others. The ambiguity of the situations, leaving basic questions unanswered, a page from a tale rather than the tale complete, add to the poems' dramatic tensions.

Stevens highlights the drama of perception—the interaction of the mind and the world, the self and the other—thematically, of course, but also stylistically, in diction and imagery and form. Since the process of interaction involved constant change, and change implies dissolution, themes of process and dissolution merge in these poems. The union is announced even on the level of vocabulary: "flash," "flick," "fleck," "flow," "whirlpool," "dissolve," all suggest movement. The use of the present participle, as in "glittering" and "twisting," implies a continuing present, but it is one that is always on the verge of disappearing into the past, "vanishing-vanished." Consonant with this motion, one image fades into another within the poems: in "Auroras VI" for example, the theatre becomes a cloud, then rock, then water, then waves of light, all within the first few lines. In the aurora borealis, as many critics have noted, Stevens discovers his most magnificently appropriate image of change. But he has others: images of fire and stars as glittering belts, the river as an image of flux and, foreshadowing the great poem of his last year, "To an Old Philosopher in Rome," the image of the threshold or doorway, that pivotal point of transformation. Even his central metaphor of the rock, as much at the still point of the turning world as anything in Stevens, is constantly transformed. The mystical language associated with these images—crown, cabala, angels—gives death and destruction a visionary status, a kind of grandeur of the end.

Yet even as Stevens's poems gulp after formlessness, they seek form. They are grouped in couplets and tercets and even more elaborate architechtural schemes. And within the cinematographic motion, Stevens manages to still the action. In a subtly interwoven moment of stasis and movement in "Auroras I," for instance, he slows the line with heavy sounding "o" and "u" monosyllables while moving the line forward with a light "i" sound so that the slight motion of the snake is described by the sound of the words: "he moved so slightly to make sure of sun" (p. 411). In other ways, Stevens deftly stills the movement by his use of pause, particularly the use of ellipsis, as in the line "It is

the earth itself that is humanity . . ." in "World without Peculiarity" (p. 454). This device is unusual in Stevens; instead of
elaborating, offering his usual appositive series, Stevens here
leaves the thought unfinished and therefore open. The final
effect, though, is peculiarly thought-suspending, so that we do
not consider other possibilities but dwell on the one Stevens
leaves us.

Stevens most clearly focuses our feeling with the sharp pho-
tographing of objects within the swirling atmospheres of the
poems. As if being observed for the last time, objects are
painted with vividness and clarity of detail: roses are "bright" in
sunlight or prick us with their most "coiled thorn"; a "black
glove" holds a "novel by Camus." Coordinating conjunctions
outline different images or concepts, giving each equal and
separate weight: "the color of ice and fire and solitude," "the
stains / And the rust and rot of the door." The repetition of
grammatical structures in parallel phrasing also establishes a
sense of ground in Stevens's changing cosmos, a position of
permanence in impermanence. Repetitions of words highlight
sensuous apprehension: "The red ripeness of round leaves is
thick / With the spices of red summer." Such lines, heavy with
repetition of both words and sounds, carry with them the
burden of nostalgia for the earth and root our attention there.

From Stevens's unusual responsiveness to things of this world
the drama of these poems unfolds. In such earlier pieces of
"Sunday Morning," the lyric hymn to the earthly paradise of
berries ripening, deer walking the mountains, and quail whis-
tling, and in his apostrophe to the globe as a "fat girl, terrestrial,
my summer, my night," Stevens registers his keen love of the
earth; but it is especially in the later poems, with the insignificant made significant by the fact of imminent death, that Stevens's emotional response to the earth is most accessible to us.
In the Ransom essay, Stevens goes on to explain how

> trivial things often touch us intensely . . . the sight of an old berry
> patch, a new growth in the spring, the particular things on display
> at a farmers' market, as, for example, the trays of poor apples, the
> few boxes of black-eyed peas, the bags of dried corn, have an
> emotional power over us that for a moment is more than we can
> control. [*OP*, p. 260]

We must, Stevens insists, acknowledge our emotional indebted-
ness to things and recognize the great hold the nonhuman has

on our human emotions as we become more and more conscious of the world around us.

The drama of consciousness, and especially of memory, is played with Stevens's fullest passion in "The Auroras of Autumn." The title sets the tone for the book as a whole: auroras—dawn, beginning; autumn—ending. But it is the fear of ending, of death—and at the same time almost a desire for it—that strikes the note the book revolves around. The idea of loss of the earth itself, the cessation of sense and thought, initiates the "season of memory" that colors all of Stevens's remaining poems. *Auroras* struggles with the questions of knowledge and consciousness that the idea of death raises—of what and how we know, even where we know, and of the uses of memory—in almost all the poems of the volume. The title poem offers a tightly focused musing of these obscurities, and "An Ordinary Evening in New Haven" issues a series of parabolic and philosophical elaborations on them. But between the extended meditations of the longer works, the shorter poems function as musical and dramatic interludes providing changes in style and perspective. "Page from a Tale" and "The Novel" offer brief narratives; "Our Stars Come from Ireland" and "Imago," folksong-like lyrics; "Puella Parvula," high romantic lyric about the mind's confrontation with the world; "Questions Are Remarks," dispassionate statement. Some poems are quite clever in conception—the personification of St. John's back-ache, for example—and even humorous, as in "The Ultimate Poem Is Abstract." In most of these poems, however, there is little of the play we have come to expect from Stevens's previous work. And although many of these shorter poems move through fear or bitterness or resignation toward a more positive vision, the overall tone is one of melancholy. Several of the poems, moreover, are extremely stark as they confront death directly and display their terror of the void death creates.

All these late poems suggest, as "Metaphor as Degeneration" is bold to say, that "being / Includes death and the imagination" (p. 444). In the starker poems in *Auroras*, the imagination is death. Thus, although early lines in "The Novel" insist that the imagination creates being—"The fire burns as the novel taught it how"—(p. 458), the poem finally concludes that the mind, acknowledging death, also creates death: "one trembles . . . / To understand, as if to know became / The fatality of seeing things too well" (p. 459). Significantly, the novel referred to is one by

Camus: as the philosopher of nothingness, he is, certainly, the appropriately chosen figure to haunt this poem.

This same sense of the absurd lingers in another poem that also contemplates the void. In "The Countryman" a figure walks beside the river thinking of death: "He broods of neither cap nor cape, / But only of your swarthy motion, / But always of the swarthy water, / Of which Swatara is the breathing, / The name" (pp. 428–29). The protagonist, declares the speaker, is thinking neither of the source nor the mouth (the "cap" and "cape"), neither of the origin nor the end of being, but of being itself.[5] But the words "Swatara," "swarthy," "heavy" and "black," repeated throughout the poem, insist on the fact of death, or on life that is conditioned by death, in sound as well as imagery. The controlled, even tone of the speaker and the control the protagonist demonstrates do not suffice to cover the blank fear that surfaces in the fixation on the river and the overly-emphatic repetitions.

Less dark than "The Countryman," two other short poems, "In a Bad Time" and "Beginning," explore the sense of tragedy beneath the quotidian. "In a Bad Time" examines, as does "Auroras," the northern lights but defines them by analogy as a symbol of our life's poverty and misery only. A tone of impending loss, of life chiseled to the fact of death, informs the poem:

> How mad would he have to be to say, "He beheld
> An order and thereafter he belonged
> To it?" He beheld the order of the northern sky.
>
> But the beggar gazes on calamity
> And thereafter belongs to it, to bread
> Hard found, and water tasting of misery.

[P. 426]

The quiet resignation, the flat statement and distanced, third-person narration only superficially mask the deep-scarred feeling in the poem: "For him cold's glacial beauty is his fate" (p. 426). Objective, factual, almost toneless, chilled as it is, this line yet betrays a restless yearning the poem cannot conquer. Stevens goes on to assert that "the heart's strong core" lies in poverty, in change and death; but to emphasize this, he must take the poem in a totally different direction. Addressing Melpomene, the muse of tragedy, in the closing stanza, Stevens commands her to discard misery and "Speak loftier lines" (p. 427). The poem thus ends not with a consideration of the way things are, but with a desire for change. Nonetheless, it does imply, in its address to Melpomene, a larger perspective on human life and suffering.

"The Beginning," similar to "In a Bad Time," begins with loss. It contrasts, simply and painfully, what is—an empty house, a rotting doorframe, an empty chair—with what was—a woman before the mirror, combing her "dewy hair, a touchless light" (p. 427). Each image of the poem—house, mirror, chair, even the birds in the last lines that begin to sing, thereby ending the tragedy—highlights the loss of summer gone, of life gone:

> This is the chair from which she gathered up
> Her dress, the carefulest, commodious weave
>
> Inwoven by a weaver to twelve bells . . .
> The dress is lying, cast-off, on the floor.
>
> Now, the first tutoyers of tragedy
> Speak softly, to begin with, in the eaves.
>
> [P. 428]

In such poems, the past cannot be regained through memory as it is regained, finally, in "The Auroras of Autumn," and death seems to claim dominion after all. This leads Stevens to the overt statement of his desire for stasis. In "This Solitude of Cataracts" the protagonist, like the figure in "The Countryman," walks along a river. Here, however, the river is not the river of death but, "flecked" as it is, the river of life. Yet the poem concentrates on "fixing" the river, stilling it. A series of parallel clauses helps create, with repetitions that effect a structural stasis, a note of longing for a changeless existence:

> He wanted to feel the same way over and over.
>
> He wanted the river to go on flowing the same way,
> To keep on flowing. He wanted to walk beside it,
>
> Under the buttonwoods, beneath a moon nailed fast.
> He wanted his heart to stop beating and his mind to rest
>
> In a permanent realization . . .
> . . . just to know how it would be,

Just to know how it would feel, released from destruction.

[P. 425]

The desire to be released from death is movingly articulated here, but a playful diction and alliteration at the end betray a touch of irony in the poem: the speaker imagines the protagonist as a "bronze man," statuelike, immobile, "breathing under archaic lapis, / Without the oscillations of planetary passpass, / Breathing his bronzen breath at the azury centre of time" (p. 425). These lines, even with their great hero-figure, then, mock the vision of stasis even as they yearn for an immortal existence.

In "The Ultimate Poem Is Abstracct," the tone is mocking from the beginning. The speaker parodies a lecturer on "This Beautiful World Of Ours," imitating the circular argument of academic discourse: "The particular question—here / The particular answer to the particular question / Is not in point" (p. 429). Yet at the end the speaker drops his ironic stance to speak plainly, and with a note of longing, of the possibility of eternal, unchanging existence: "It would be enough / If we were ever, just once, at the middle, fixed / In This Beautiful World Of Ours and not as now, / Helplessly at the edge" (p. 430).

Yet if several of these short poems trail off into a melancholy desire for the unattainable, several others conclude with assertions of faith in reality. "Celle Qui Fût Héaulmiette" also explores the theme of an immutable world, but ends by singing the satisfactions of mutability. The protagonist, desiring a whole world, an "unbroken circle / Of summer" (p. 438), manufactures shields to protect her against change. Yet at the end of the poem she finds fulfillment in the bright and dying earth, "Entinselled and gilderlinged and gone" (p. 438), which she accepts as her true "shield." In this poem about unfulfilled desire, Stevens shows why desire need not be satisfied as expected in order to be satisfied.

Other poems support the view that Stevens's desire for stasis is a momentary desire only, usually overcome. "World without peculiarity" begins bleakly contrasting life and death, but then moves through despondence to an affirmation of life lived full in the knowledge of death. A series of contradictions introduced by "But" gives the poem its structural and emotional tension:

> The day is great and strong—
> But his father was strong, that lies now
> In the poverty of dirt.

> [P. 453]

The first stanza views the world as alien to us, a place of separation and peculiarity. The image of the grave leads into other lines suggesting loss:

> Nothing could be more hushed than the way
> The moon moves toward the night.
> But what his mother was returns and cries on his breast.
>
> The red ripeness of round leaves is thick
> With the spices of red summer.
> But she that he loved turns cold at his light touch.

> [P. 453]

The completeness of each of the stanzas emphasizes the final separateness of death; the sensuousness of the red leaves only underscores their ephemerality. Neither does love last, as "she that he loved turns cold." The memories of father, mother, and lover, now dead, raise the question, bitter and despairing in the middle stanza: "What good is it that the earth is justified, / That it is complete, that it is an end, / That in itself it is enough?" (p. 453). The act of asking the question, however, provides the impetus for the turning point in the speaker's attitude. His response breaks totally his earlier self-pitying stance: "It is the earth itself that is humanity . . ." (p. 454). And here, Stevens's careful placing of the pause allows time for this radical response to be absorbed before elaborating that "He is the inhuman son and she, / She is the fateful mother, whom he does not know" (p. 454). The son is inhuman because he fails to acknowledge the earth, constantly changing, as his parent, intimately related to him. (Here again Stevens is taming the world, as he did earlier in "Auroras.") Only by seeking identity with the physical world, Stevens seems to be saying, will differences or "peculiarity" disappear, and the seeming meaninglessness of our lives acquire meaning:

> She is the day, the walk of the moon
> Among the breathless spices and, sometimes,
> He, too, is human and difference disappears

And the poverty of dirt, the thing upon his breast,
The hating woman, the meaningless place,
Become a single being, sure and true.

[P. 454]

This imaginative transformation of death into life, of the earth from a grave into a desired woman, is the focus of all but the most negative of the poems in *Auroras*. In several of the poems Stevens lends his idea emotional force through a dramatic technique of contrasting voices. Both "Imago" and "Page from a Tale," for example, infuse an alien voice into the poem. "Imago" establishes in the first lines the reality of postwar Europe, of France no longer France, Britain buried, Germany sunk under the weight of its destruction. Yet the poem immediately prescribes as cure the imagination, the "image":

Who can pick up the weight of Britain,
Who can move the German load
Or say to the French here is France again?
Imago. Imago. Imago.

[P. 439]

Stevens is also playing with the scientific meaings of the word *imago* (the third state of insects—accordning to Linnaeus—in which they attain their proper shape and color; the representation in childhood, according to Freud, of the adult human being).[6] The middle stanzas then place, very simply, ordinary man at the center of imagination's power: it is the normal or "Medium man" who "hears the imagination's hymns / And sees its images" (p. 439). But the last lines, set in italics apart from the rest, qualify the assertions of the mind's puissance. The shift from the present indicative to the imperative mood, from accomplishment to desire, stresses this qualification: "*Lightly and lightly, O my land, / Move lightly through the air again*" (p. 439). The note of longing, in contrast to the authoritative voice at the end of "World without Peculiarity," closes the poem, and reverberates back through it.

"Page from a Tale" draws a similarly ambiguous situation in which the imagination, set up as a counter to the chaos and destruction of the world, is then seriously questioned. The situation the poem presents—of a figure Hans sitting by a

driftwood fire beside a frozen sea, gazing on a ship newly
foundered in the ice—is unclear (p. 421). Who is Hans? Why is
he on the ice? Remembered snatches of Yeats's "Lake Isle of
Innisfree" evoke images of spring and escape; woven into the
bleakness of the winter scene, they relieve its enforced isolation.
At the beginning of the poem, then, the two worlds of harsh
reality and the beneficent imagination contend with each other.
In the second stanza, the two worlds begin to merge as the sea
becomes a sea José "dreamed" and the stars acquire the imagination's ability to "sing." As the poem progresses, reality grows
less and less familiar: the sun, the image for Stevens of reality,
becomes a foreign object, "no longer known" and "Beyond the
habit of sense, anarchic shape / Afire—" (p. 422). Moreover, the
sun destroys the known—much as the mind seeks to destroy
metaphor to get to the thing itself. The destruction, then, is
positive. Portending (it may or may not "speed home its por-
tents to their ends"), the sun becomes a bizarre figure for the
inhuman imagination, both self-generating and self-destroying,
capable of

> Slight gestures that could rend the palpable ice,
> Or melt Arcturus to ingots dropping drops,
> Or spill night out in brilliant vanishings.

> [P. 423]

Like the light of the aurora borealis it recalls, the light of the
sun implies a metaphysical darkness, a nothingness, as dark
and light become one:

> Whirlpools of darkness in whirlwinds of light . . .
> The miff-maff-muff of water, the vocables
> Of the wind, the glassily-sparkling particles
> Of the mind—

> [P. 423]

Significantly, it is "thought" that creates these self-consuming
gestures; the imagination, in other words, holds within itself the
knowledge and source of its own destruction: "Death and the
imagination," as we have seen before, "are one." As the imagination consumes the world in a whirlpool, language—the
poem—is itself consumed. Verbs are devoured, lines un-

finished. Matter and mind fuse in this dissolving whirlwind, and are subsumed. The last line, however, pits order and light against the chaos of darkness: the men "march single file, with electric lamps, alert / For a tital undulation underneath" (p. 423). After the whirling phrases of the previous lines, the simple syntax here provides stability and relief, and the image of the lamps functions as a familiar image of human control. But on second reading the lamps seem insignificant stays against either the darkness or the "fire aflame" of the sun; and the same fear of the scholar of one candle as he faces the auroras lingers here after the last line.

Despite this rather terrifying equation of death and the imagination, without the consolations offered in "Auroras," Stevens presents in other poems persuasive defenses of poetry as imaginative stays against destruction. Among the shorter poems, "Large Red Man Reading" and "Puella Parvula" constitute two of Stevens's most triumphant statements on the primacy of the imagination. "Large Red Man" sets the world of death against that of the imagination. (Significantly, it comes early in the volume, immediately following "Page from a Tale," which questions the mind's power). The dead, disappointed in the "wilderness of stars," come back to earth to hear the large man, mythic in stature but red with the warmth and blood of being alive, read from the book of life. The ghosts are eager to hear of the most commonplace objects, the "pans above the stove, the pots on the table, the tulips among them" (p. 423). They long for the most simple sensory contact:

They were those that would have wept to step barefoot into reality,

That would have wept and been happy, have shivered in the frost
And cried out to feel it again, have run fingers over leaves
And against the most coiled thorn.

[Pp. 423–24]

Even with the pain of the cold and of the pricking thorns, the mutable world is preferable to the eternal. And within the world, the poem asserts, it is poetry that enables us to appreciate the world. The ghosts listen to the man reading "The outlines of being and its expressings, the syllables of its law: / *Poesis, poesis*, the literal characters, the vatic lines" (p. 424). Not being itself, but the expression of being, as in poetry, is that which gives life its meaning.

"Puella Parvula" portrays the winds of decreation, of death, that have raged through the volume from their first appearance in "Auroras," subdued by the imagination. The little girl of the title is the "wild bitch" of our fear of death reduced, like the wild winds, by the "dauntless master," the imagination, to smaller stature. Stevens skillfully builds toward the climax, vividly illustrating the immense power of the winds in order to communicate more fully the power of the imagination. The opening stanza presents the scene of dissolution already witnessed in "The Auroras of Autumn," a scene of autumn winds prophesying winter: "Every thread of summer is at last unwoven. / By one caterpillar is great Africa devoured / And Gibraltar is dissolved like spit in the wind" (p. 456). The tone is quiet, but the scene frightening: our image for the most substantial thing in the world, the rock of Gibraltar, is no more lasting than spray. After this quiet though ominous opening, the poem assumes a more oracular tone as it conveys the great force of the wind. Stevens invokes the figures of beasts to aid in portraying the wind's power: he compares the wind to "The elephant on the roof and its elephantine blaring, / The bloody lion in the yard at night or ready to spring." In a truly terrifying image, Stevens figures destruction as "a vacant sea declaiming with wide throat," ready to devour. The urgent, driving force of these lines is highlighted by the suspended clauses in the long, ten-line central sentence—"over the wind, over the legends . . . Over all these." Only after he has built up this startling rhythm does Stevens introduce the imagination as a power capable of defeating the mighty winds of destruction; over these winds the "mighty imagination triumphs / Like a trumpet." The mind itself, gone wild with the weather, must be made a child again: "Keep quiet in the heart, O wild bitch. O mind / Gone wild, be what he tells you to be: *Puella*." The imagination conquers the raging, despairing side of the mind, brings it peace. Yet—and this is the poem's greatest triumph, the source of its power and courage—the imagination, though victorious, is not transcendant, not glorious. It sings no gloria in excelsis but merely a "human tale":

> Be still. The *summarium in excelsis* begins . . .
> Flame, sound, fury composed . . . Hear what he says,
> The dauntless master, as he starts the human tale.

> [P. 456]

Flame, sound, fury together compose the elements of our lives; and they can be composed, says Stevens, only by the imagination, which triumphs over death only in allowing us a peaceful acceptance of death.

Stevens's most confident assertion of imagination's value appears in *Auroras* in a difficult poem, "Reply to Papini." In it, Stevens contends that poets are our true guides through the world. Taking on Pope Celestin, who has through his procurator Papini defied the poets, he declares that "The way through the world / Is more difficult to find than the way beyond it" (p. 446). Merely to live, Stevens maintains, requires an "heroic effort . . . expressed / As victory" (p. 446). A quotation from his essay, "Imagination as Value," provides a useful gloss on the poem and on his theories of poetry and imagination in general:

> To be able to see . . . the portal of the imagination as a scene of normal love and normal beauty is, of itself, a feat of great imagination. It is the vista a man sees, seated in the public garden of his native town, near by some effigy of a figure celebrated in the normal world, as he considers that the chief problems of any artist, as of any man, are the problems of the normal and that he needs, in order to solve them, everything the imagination has to give.[7]

In the poems of *The Auroras of Autumn*, through the figures of mother and father, a man walking, a woman combing, Stevens presents the normal situations that we must accept and live through. In "Imagination as Value," he shows us the strength of mind we must develop in order to live fully, triumphantly, without bitterness or despair. Yet many of his poems in *Auroras* are tinged with regret as Stevens takes the measure of our lives and finds it wanting. Overall, the poems reveal a nostalgia for the lost world of our childhood, a past before our fall. Yet the last poem in the book qualifies even this interpretation. "Angel Surrounded by Paysans," if sentimental and overrated as some think,[8] yet breaks the heaviness of spirit that suffuses the book, and lifts the whole lightly into another realm. The angel of the poem, a figure of both reality and the imagination, standing on the threshold of an open door, puts the tragedy of our lives into larger perspective and raises us to consciousness of another life:

> Yet I am the necessary angel of earth,
> Since, in my sight, you see the earth again,

> Cleared of its stiff and stubborn, man-locked set,
> And, in my hearing, you hear its tragic drone
>
> Rise liquidly in liquid lingerings,
> Like watery words awash.

[Pp. 496–97]

Stevens extends, in these late poems, not only his own emotional range, but ours. The poems teach us to be sensitive to the "pans above the stove, the pots on the table," and, more importantly, to understand why such trivial things affect us so deeply. What the poems reveal, after their first seeming opacity, is a bold clairvoyance, a "visibility of thought." To understand Stevens is more and more to read him whole, read the whole of his harmonium as he puts the parts of his world together in his books. In *The Auroras of Autumn* we discover not someone beyond us, but of ourselves, a poet of the ordinary, of our "actual spirit" who acknowledges and records what a "heroic effort" it takes to live a normal life. The reality that Stevens writes about is, more and more in the later poetry, as much a mental or internal reality as it is an external one. But this does not make it less real. Rather, Stevens shows us how much of life is lived in the head and forces us to examine that life and discover the great value of consciousness.

Notes

1. Wallace Stevens, *Opus Posthumous*, ed. Samuel French Morse (New York: Knopf, 1957), p. 260; hereafter *OP*, with page numbers cited in the text.

2. *Letters of Wallace Stevens*, ed. Holly Stevens (New York: Knopf, 1966), p. 643.

3. For commentary on "Auroras" and "An Ordinary Evening in New Haven," see Harold Bloom, *Wallace Stevens: The Poems of Our Climate* (Ithaca, N. Y.: Cornell University Press, 1976), pp. 253–80 and 305–37; Joseph N. Riddel, *The Clairvoyant Eye: The Poetry and Poetics of Wallace Stevens* (Baton Rouge: Louisiana State University Press, 1965), pp. 235–40; and Helen Hennessy Vendler, *On Extended Wings: Wallace Stevens' Longer Poems* (Cambridge: Harvard University Press, 1969), pp. 246–305. For comments on other poems in the volume, see especially Bloom, pp. 281–304; Thomas J. Hines, *The Later Poetry of Wallace Stevens: Phenomenological Parallels with Husserl and Heidegger* (Lewisburg, Penna.: Bucknell University Press, 1976), pp. 250–66, and Riddel, pp. 224–43. I am indebted to these and other critics for my understanding of Stevens.

4. Wallace Stevens, *The Auroras of Autumn*, in *The Collected Poems of Wallace Stevens* (New York: Knopf, 1954), pp. 411–96; page references to the *Auroras* will be cited parenthetically in the text.

5. Hines, *The Later Poetry*, p. 253, helps clarify the images of "cap" and "cape" in the poem. His analysis of the river imagery in the late poems as an image of "Being" is also instructive, although I find it to be somewhat limiting. Vendler's discussion of the river imagery in "The River of Rivers in Connecticut" as a celebration of "the concurrence of all orders, both orders of magnitude and orders of relation" is more original. See *Wallace Stevens: Words Chosen Out of Desire* (Knoxville: University of Tennessee Press, 1984), pp. 72–79.

6. *The Compact Edition of the Oxford English Dictionary* (Oxford: Oxford University Press, 1971), p. 1337.

7. Wallace Stevens, *The Necessary Angel: Essays on Reality and the Imagination* (New York: Knopf, 1951), p. 156.

8. Bloom especially objects to this poem, which he finds "sentimentally evasive enough to have become fairly popular." See *Wallace Stevens*, p. 304.

The Problem of Indeterminacy in Stevens

Terrance King
Wayne State University

A reader of Wallace Stevens has to confront not only the obscurity of his verse but also a recurring contradiction involved with the handling of this obscurity. On one hand the poetry invites us to struggle with its enigmas and thereby participate in the poet's own vigorous act of poesis. His point that "it is necessary to propose an enigma to the mind"[1] and his view that poetry "must give pleasure"[2] express only different sides of the same principle. But in other ways, his writing also warns us not to feel that we could ever win this struggle in the sense of our solving the riddles of the poem in some kind of conclusive fashion. For to a modernist like Stevens, to "solve" a poem—or rather from his point of view, to *think* one has done so—is to destroy its whole purpose. "As soon as people are perfectly sure of a poem," he declares in a letter, "they are just as likely as not to have no further interest in it; it loses whatever potency it had."[3] We are asked to apply the intelligence with a force akin to that of the poet's own intelligence, and yet at the same time we are to maintain a kind of strategic ignorance, for as Stevens's own paradox puts it, "the poem reveals itself only to the ignorant man" (*OP*, p. 160). In one sense his point is obvious and inarguable: if a poem is treated solely as a puzzle that has already been solved, it offers no joy of challenge. But such a point does not really show that a riddle-poem, presuming it could be solved, would lose all interest on other grounds. Neither does it demonstrate that the enigmas in Stevens's own verse are irresolvable.

Of course once one agrees with Stevens's own modernist point that the life and renewability of a poem depend upon its obscurity, its resistance, then it seems natural enough to infer that Stevens, in a deliberate effort to assure the renewability of his own poetry, creates riddles without answers and thereby builds a kind of wall of indeterminacy within the structure of the poem itself. Since most of his commentators still share his own modernist assumptions, they tend to believe that there in fact is such a wall and that anyone attempting to scale it would be guilty of crass reductionism. In a general sense this assumption is tacitly expressed by the widespread avoidance of any question that would squarely address the issue of Stevens's obscurity. And when the problem is mentioned at all, it is generally dubbed irrelevant or irresolvable. As when Helen Vendler makes clearance for her stylistic study, *On Extended Wings*, by yawning away the whole issue of the poet's ideas. "Abstractly considered," she observes, "Stevens' 'themes' are familiar, not to say, banal ones."[4] And in a centennial essay on Stevens, J. Hillis Miller—whose approach to literature little resembles Vendler's in other ways—speaks in an almost religious vein about the necessity for indeterminacy in poetry:

> The moment when the poem ceases to resist the intelligence and can be "seen through" theoretically may be the moment when the poem fails. It then fails any longer to bring a relation, even figurative to . . . the essential poem at the center of things, which may be neither named, nor seen, nor possessed, theoretically.[5]

Perhaps the most explicit of all, however, is Frank Doggett, who recommends that we read Stevens's verse as poetry involving "an area of meaning rather than one certain meaning," because Stevens's ideas "are usually only half developed, as well as only half revealed."[6] Doggett in fact is quite contemptuous of one's even considering the possibility that the poet has something up his sleeve. "Certainly Stevens," he says, "never thought that in an implication there was one certain meaning hidden in the act of creating it—the poem's sealed letter to the reader, to be opened by the poet or some ideal intuitive critic."[7]

In opposition to all this, I want to argue not only that Stevens's enigmas can be resolved but that, once resolved, they reveal a deliberate strategy of secrecy on his part. Even though a certain kind of indeterminacy exists in poetry, I am going to argue at the end of this paper that it is not the type critics like the above attribute to Stevens. In this short paper, I can't hope to prove an argument like this, but I can at least sketch the outlines of what such a demonstration would entail and what one of its implications might be.

In my earlier writings on Stevens, I propose that there is in his poetry from 1917 onward a nearly pervasive subject he himself calls a "poetry of words" (*OP*, p. 163), a self-reflexive theme in which the words of a poem talk about themselves in a most literal sense, a sense that is in fact so obvious that, like Poe's purloined letter, it eludes our far-sighted expectations.[8] On one hand Stevens creates a surface that poses paradoxes and other enigmas of various kinds, although it is still a surface that succeeds in creating an unmistakable reference to a world external to the poem, an elsewhere of scenes and people—a Florida, a Rome, a New Haven, a Bucks County. And yet at the same time these enigmas can be resolved again and again by our recognizing a poetry "without external reference" (*CP*, p. 251), by our treating the scenes and people, not primarily as representing an elsewhere (the actual Florida, Rome, etc.), but as allegorizations of a semiotic conception in which the words of a poem literally talk about themselves and their own power of representation. In "Autumn Refrain" we find the phrase "the moon and moon" (*CP*, p. 160), which at first glance seems to be mere nonsense but which self-reflexively refers to the double nature of the word taken as a sign, a vehicle of representation: the word as its referent (in this case the moon) and the word simply as itself ("moon"). In "The Man on the Dump" the last line poses the question, "Where was it one first heard of the truth?" (*CP*, p. 203), followed by the enigmatic answer, "the the," which may be read as a reference to the word "the" and by implication all the words of language, including the word "truth," of which "the" would be a demonstrative in a double sense. By itself alone, this kind of sleight of hand is a triviality, true enough, but for Stevens it points to something quite crucial. In a nihilistic age such as the one in which the poet finds himself, language seems to prove everything false, and yet not quite everything: the power of language to represent a world of truth and then, through this same power, subvert this world— this power itself cannot be false. And poetry, with its overt fictionality (telling you its illusions are *only* illusions), is the vehicle par excellence for representing this power of representation.

For the sake of comparison, let us see how Doggett treats the enigmas in a poem like Stevens's "The Creations of Sound." In the following discussion from his *Wallace Stevens: The Making of the Poem*, in which he cites a portion of this lyric, notice that a key part of a clause, which I have italicized, is omitted:

> *There are words*
> Better without an author, without a poet,
>
> Or having a separate author, a different poet,
> An accretion from ourselves, intelligent
> Beyond intelligence, an artificial man
>
> At a distance, a secondary expositor,
> A being of sound, whom one does not approach
> Through any exaggeration. From him we collect.

> In "The Creations of Sound," Stevens is concerned almost entirely with the theory of the involuntary imagination. Many contradictory statements of his about the source of poetry can be considered as emanating from a bias for one or the other conception of the nature of creativity, as when he wrote Latimer that "writing poetry is conscious activity. While poems may very well occur, they had very much better be caused."[9]

Unlike many Stevens commentators, Doggett at least sees the contradictoriness of the poet's verse as an important feature, and, also to his credit, he accounts for this feature on thematic and not just stylistic grounds. But the problem here is that his reading of this Stevens passage as an affirmation of the involuntary imagination does little to explain the actual enigmas in the passage. Presumably, with his assumption that Stevens's ideas are "only half developed, as well as only half revealed," we are to let the enigmas lie in their cloud of indeterminacy.

But the obscurity of the passage derives, not from actual indeterminacy, but from outright deception. Stevens is shrewdly aware that modernism—although he would not call it that—keeps some parts of Romanticism even though it defines itself against others; and he knows that his modernist readers will, in true Romanticist fashion, thematize the poem around the figure of the poet, especially his creative psyche (notice that Doggett's leading oppositional categories are all psychologizing—rational/irrational, voluntary/involuntary, conscious/unconscious). He knows very well that his readers will identify "The Creations of Sound" with the poet even though he warns them here quite baldly that "there are words / Better without an author, without a poet." Doggett omits the first part of the clause, "there are words," but as it turns out, the poem is literally about its own words. Consider the following opposition:

The voice of the poem as that of its originator (i.e., the historical figure, Wallace Stevens)	vs.	The voice of the poem as that of the text (i.e., the words themselves here and now under your performance)

Using the right-hand version, you find that as you read the poem, the words create Wallace Stevens, who in this strict linguistic framework is not a human being (that would be an "exaggeration") but a conception evoked by the words, "an artificial man / At a distance, a secondary expositor," who is literally a "being of sound." In this most literal sense, the words themselves speak to you in the first person "we" as their own chorus-persona: they tell you that it is better without an author, without a poet. They—the words right in front of you—are the poet for the moment, or if a different poet is to be considered (i.e., Wallace Stevens), he must be conceived as only an "accretion" from these words. The poem of words, which is intelligent beyond the intelligence of the poet, is thus the creator whenever it is performed by anyone, be it Wallace Stevens as he writes it or any reader at any subsequent moment of the text's history. But since the intelligence of the language is the intelligence of the performer, all three—the poem's language, the poet, and the reader—are here made equivalent terms, with the result that personal pronouns like "we" and "him" are made to refer ambiguously to all three. But the key ambiguity in this riddle-poem lies in the preposition "of" in the title, "The Creations of Sound": obviously poems are creations *in* sound, but the things of which they speak—including even the poet—are creations *by* sound.

The conflict here with Doggett over this particular poem illustrates my more general disagreement with him and many other Stevens commentators. In sum, I am arguing that the enigmas in Stevens's verse are not inscrutable, and the thought they reveal is anything but undeveloped and indeterminate. This view is not incompatible with the fact that a poem functions as an ambiguous play of different meanings rather than— as in the tendency of prose—a univocal assertion of a single meaning, for as we have just seen, awareness of the poetry of words in a Stevens poem actually depends upon an understanding of how ambiguity can "play" in a lyric. Ambiguity, in short, is not the same thing as indeterminacy. And yet it might well be asked whether Doggett is still not right in a more general sense. Are there not more themes in Stevens than just his poetry of words? And are there not other ways of reading him than just this one way? And if so, can't we, like Doggett, read a Stevens poem as having "an area of meaning rather than one certain meaning"? I am not suggesting that the poetry of words is the only theme in a Stevens poem (even though the secrecy enveloping it seems to make it paramount). I am suggesting simply that indeterminacy cannot be blithely attributed to the poet's obscurity. Textual indeterminacy does not depend ipso facto on whether a text is ambiguous or univocal, poetic or prosaic, obscure or lucid, sublime or banausic, or any other quality immanent to it; it depends rather on its interaction with the institution that through history keeps interpreting it. There cannot be a definitive reading of "The Creations of Sound" for the same reason there cannot be one of the Constitution or the Book of Revelation: such texts are in a dialogue as it were with the commentaries continually being generated by their respective institutions. The commentary, as one of the "interlocutors," has a crucial institutional role in the creation of textual information: it selects the point of view, ordains the hierarchies of topic, defines the relevant contexts, establishes the demarcations between figurative and literal, ironic and nonironic, etcetera. The poetry of Stevens must, therefore, be indeterminate in this sociohistorical sense of an ongoing dialogue, but not necessarily in the fixed and immanent sense Doggett and so many others attribute to it. In fact the modernist myth of the autonomous poem standing by itself as a timeless plenitude of meaning could well be the incentive inducing so many readers of Stevens's verse to equate one of its immanent qualities—namely, its obscurity—with indeterminacy.

Notes

1. Wallace Stevens, *Opus Posthumous*, ed. Samuel French Morse (New York: Knopf, 1957), p. 168; hereafter *OP*, with page references cited in the text.

2. Wallace Stevens, *The Collected Poems of Wallace Stevens* (New York: Knopf, 1954), p. 398; hereafter *CP*, with page references cited in the text.

3. Wallace Stevens, *Letters of Wallace Stevens*, ed. Holly Stevens (New York: Knopf, 1966), p. 294; hereafter *L*, with page references cited in the text.

4. Helen Hennessy Vendler, *On Extended Wings: Wallace Stevens' Longer Poems* (Cambridge: Harvard University Press, 1969), p. 13.

5. J.Hillis Miller, "Theoretical and Atheoretical in Stevens," *Wallace Stevens: A Celebration*, ed. Frank Doggett and Robert Buttel (Princeton, N.J.: Princeton University Press, 1980), p. 285.

6. Frank Doggett, *Wallace Stevens: The Making of the Poem* (Baltimore, Md.: Johns Hopkins University Press, 1980), pp. 65–66 and 42.

7. Ibid., pp. 44–45.

8. Terrance King, "'Certain Phenomena of Sound': An Illustration of Wallace Stevens' Poetry of Words," *Texas Studies in Literature and Language* 20 (1978): 599–614; "The Semiotic Poetry of Wallace Stevens," *Semiotica* 23 (1978): 78–98; review of *Wallace Stevens: The Making of the Poem*, by Frank Doggett, *Criticism* 22 (1980): 400–407. My *Semiotica* essay gives a general exposition of the poetry of words, and the *TSLL* article illustrates it with an in-depth analysis of a single poem. For discussions of how this idea opposes the Romanticist, author-centered mode of reading Stevens, see my review of Doggett's book in *Criticism* and Part II of my review of *The Southern Review*'s special centennial issue on the poet in *The Wallace Stevens Journal* 4 (1980): 27–32. Much of my discussion of "The Creations of Sound" in this present paper is taken from the Doggett review.

9. Doggett, *Wallace Stevens*, pp. 18–19.

Marianne Moore's "Marriage": Lexis and Structure

Rosanne Wasserman

Pace University

A MONG the corpus of Marianne Moore's difficult poetry, the piece "Marriage" is particularly complex, well armored in gorgeous abstractions and dazzling transitions. Its structure depends upon a quest for definition of marriage. But clues as to the nature of this definition are buried under Moore's ornate decoration, crazy-quilt quotations, and her protean ironic tone. To follow Moore's meaning, the reader must attend to lexis: not only to the familiar rhetorics of transition and addition that hold her borrowings in proximity, but to the weight of repetition and synonymity as ironic overtones develop; not only to the eccentric vocabulary, contributing gusto, but also to the smaller, ambiguously simple words that shift and change through pressure of position. The poem is in itself a difficult marriage, its elements united through the linear process of reading and the structure of making sense of what is read, but always suffering disjunction due to the complexity and multiplicity of detail.

First published in 1923, "Marriage" consists, as Moore says, of "statements that took my fancy which I tried to arrange plausibly."[1] But the 295 lines[2] challenge the reader to discover the plausibility of so engaging and distracting a surface. Few readers will deny William Carlos Williams's appraisal of the poem's clarity of design, which renders the quotational context scarcely noticeable.[3] But it is not immediately apparent what elements lend clarity to Moore's voice, which is continually in

156

danger of becoming dark through the meanders of her argument. Certainly, there is a structure of words themselves that provides interior outline and ulterior connective in Moore's richly inlaid mosaic and permits the poem to finally achieve an ironically indefinite definition of marriage.

Moore's set of terms for marriage progresses from one-word propositions modified by paradox, to metaphor and allegory, to set speeches and ironic quotes from oratory. Although the word "marriage" itself does not enter the poem until line 123, of prime importance is its appearance as the title. Without that key, the poem would remain a riddle, unself-defined. In a world where a *speragmos* is the response to beauty—"it tears one to pieces" (l. 39), says Moore, echoing H. D.[4]—how define marriage? Moore and her two main characters, Adam and Eve, propose and reject terms throughout the poem, but the fixity of the title is not unlike the fixed Daniel Webster statue at the end: a simple given, impossibly true, unutterably false. The struggle to be two as one is encapsulated in the words themselves, as for example when Adam replies to Eve's demand for quiet *à la* Garbo:

> "I should like to be alone";
> to which the visitor replies,
> "*I* should like to be alone;
> why not be alone together?"

> [ll. 31–34]

Is one alone all-one or a-lone? Is being alone together (all-one two-gether) tantamount to marriage? And if so, is it possible?

Beside its effort to describe the marriage of Adam and Eve, the poem attempts to marry the diverse materials that Moore borrowed from the languages of science, religion, imagist and symbolist poets, classical myths and the Bible, stage and Hollywood, ironist and orator. In the *Complete Poems*, she lists two pages of sources for "Marriage," from Francis Bacon to Ezra Pound (pp. 271–73). Her first definition of marriage as institution arose in a conversation with Alfred Stieglitz, recorded only in one of her notebooks.[5] Not a few of the key terms suggested for marriage are embedded in these bits and pieces, arranged by Moore as plausibly as possible, as a matchmaker arranges the village's available couples.

The most common alternative terms for marriage in this list

MARRIAGE

This *institution*

[perhaps one should say . . .]   enterprise   [out of respect for which one says one
                                                         need not change one's mind about a thing
                                                         one has believed in]

                                     . . . private *obligation*

[I wonder what Adam and Eve   *it*   [by this time]
think of]

                                     this fire-gilt *steel* alive with
                                     goldenness

[how bright . . .]   *it*   [shows]

                                                         [of circular traditions and impostures,
                                                         committing many spoils]

                                                         [requiring all one's criminal ingenuity to
                                                         avoid!]

                                     that first crystal-fine *experiment*

                                     this *amalgamation* [which can never be more than . . .]

                                     . . . an interesting *impossibility*

(EVE) [describing . . .]   *it*

[as]   "that strange *paradise*   [unlike flesh, gold, or stately buildings]

                                     the choicest *piece* of my life

[the heart rising on its . . .]   *estate* of peace   [as a boat rises with the rising of the water]

(ADAM) [has prophesied correctly;] the industrious *waterfall*

                                     "the speedy *stream* [which violently bears all before . . .]

                                     . . . *it,*   [at one time silent as the air and now as
                                                         powerful as the wind"]

                                     "past *states*, the present *state*, *seals*,
                                     promises, the *evil* one suffered, the
                                     good one enjoys, *hell, heaven*,
                                     everything convenient to promote
                                     one's joy"

(ADAM) [he stumbles over . . .]   *marriage*

                                     "a very trivial *object* indeed"   [to have disturbed the attitude in which he
                                                                        stood]

                                     that *experiment* of Adam's with ways
                                     out but no ways in

                                     the *ritual* of marriage

                                     "Married people   [often look that way"—seldom and cold,
                                                         up and down, mixed and malarial, with a
                                                         good day and a bad."]

[One sees that . . .]   *it*   [is rare]

                                     that striking *grasp* of opposites
                                     opposed each to the other

[not to . . .]   unity   [which in cycloid inclusiveness has
                                                         dwarfed the demonstration of Colombus
                                                         with the egg]

                                     a *triumph* of simplicity

                                     that charitive *Euroclydon*   [of frightening disinterestedness]

                                                                    [which the world hates]

[which says, I have encountered . . .]*it*

are "it," used six times, "experiment," used twice, and "state," which appears twice, echoing "estate." Among the significant modifiers are "this" and "that"; "this" begins the poem, but "that" takes over from it in frequency as definition begins to distance Moore from her subject. Of the remaining nouns, "institution," "enterprise," and "obligation" suggest the social aspects of marriage; "amalgamation" and "impossibility" work with "experiment" to invoke the scientific and philosophical; Godwin's "trivial object" is a direct lifting from the social philosopher. The "fire-gilt steel" and the "waterfall" may be read as paradoxical metaphors for marriage: the steel, "alive with goldenness" and punning on "of circular traditions" creates by indirection an image of the golden wedding ring; Adam's waterfall, further described as a "speedy stream," violent, silent, and powerful, stands in contrast, if not in contradiction, to Eve's vision of marriage as an "estate of peace" on which the heart rises as a boat floats, securely at anchor. Also illustrative of the two visions at odds are "that strange paradise" not to be compared to the worldly treasures that men monopolize (not only "flesh, gold, and stately buildings," but "stars, garters, buttons, and other shining baubles," ll. 205–6); and the "past states" speech in which both evil and good, heaven and hell, are considered as part of those necessities to promote one's joy, along with the seals and promises that figure so largely in the ritual of marriage.

The word "one" occurs no less than twenty-two times in the poem, only once as an adjective. This repetition is a counterpart to the theme of unity in marriage, stressing the singleness of persons. "One" may refer to any member of a conventional society, who might escape its strictures through personal effort: "requiring public promises / of one's intention / to fulfil a private obligation" (ll. 6–8); "requiring all one's criminal ingenuity to avoid!" (ll. 16–17). "One" also refers to the author's impersonalization of her own perception, usually appearing with verbs of naming: "perhaps one should say enterprise" (l. 2); "one must not call him ruffian / nor friction a calamity" (ll. 157–58). In addition, "one" has its familiar neutral grammaticality as Eve's or Adam's rhetorical persona: "the evil one suffered, the good one enjoys" (ll. 92–93); "What can one do with it?" (l. 228). Later Moore echoes Eve's question, referring to both Adam and Eve after coolly appraising Eve's behavior in terms of the single person:

one is not rich but poor
when one can always seem so right.
What can one do for them—
these savages condemned to disaffect
all those who are not visionaries
alert to the silly task
of making people noble?

[ll. 247–54]

In opposition, again, to the savage in "Marriage," the original natives of the planet, Adam and Eve, Moore posits an "all," a social *monde*, evoked elsewhere primarily through her use of "we" and "us." The penultimate speech in the poem is given to the world itself, which hates marriage but is a unified diversity; which speaks in the first person singular; and which uses "one" for the last time in the poem, excluding itself from a certain group of individuals capable of marriage:

"I am not one of those
who have a great sorrow
in the morning
and a great joy at noon."

[ll. 277–80]

This is the kind of paradox that Moore rejoices in: it permits her to be as complex as she liked to be, while letting her remain only as clear as her reticence allowed her to be.[6] Her attention to the possibilities inherent in the simplest terms helps her to layer ironies, to structure paradoxes, within the multiple movements of the poem.

There are many more examples of the ways Moore uses repetition, synonyms, and simple words to structure and to order the more gorgeous and gaudy language of this poem, but it is worthwhile, too, to examine more unusual words as well as the common ones, especially as they gain force and meaning through the pressures of interplay. One example will suffice to illustrate. Toward the end of "Marriage," the last noun describing or defining her subject is "Euroclydon," a biblical storm that caused Paul's ship to wreck upon Melita (Malta) in Acts 27:14. The wreck permits Paul and his fellow Christians to escape from their Roman captors, swimming to freedom or clinging to the fragments of the wreck. Moore shows both comic and ironic subtlety in choosing Euroclydon, a force both destructive and preserving, as an epithet for marriage. Her irony lies especially in naming marriage as the power that splinters the institution—for the ship in this episode came to be associated with the Church itself—rather than as the institution itself, to whose fragments some of the faithful still cling. Thus she reverses her initial definition, "this institution" of line 1.

The whirlwind Euroclydon must not be confused with powerful emotion: Moore does not mean to name love or passion as a "charitive Euroclydon." The adjective "charitive" reveals the intellectual nature of this force and of marriage, which has in fact all the "frightening disinterestedness" of something fully rational. It is Adam's abstraction, Eve's pure sensuality, that are irrational. Paul, like Adam, has prophesied correctly, but fails to recognize the nature of his salvation, for those who abided in the ship were not in fact saved that way; at last they too would have to swim for it. Eve, who also misinterprets Euroclydon, seeing only the boat rising gently on an "estate of peace," is linked in the poem with Peter, when Moore calls her "this model of Petrine fidelity / who 'leaves her peaceful husband / only because she has seen enough of him'" (ll. 255–57)—denying her lord and master, bored with "the choicest piece" of her life.

No wonder that the world, confused by such complexity, hates the destructive but charitive Euroclydon, that disturbing power that frees people from impending slavery to the consequences of their actions, but only by means of tossing them into the drink. The world's defeated confession, in colloquial and homey terms, has nevertheless its own biblical ring:

> "I am such a cow,
> if I had a sorrow,
> I should feel it a long time;
> I am not one of those
> who have a great sorrow
> in the morning
> and a great joy at noon."

[ll. 274–80]

The last speaker in the poem is difficult to identify, as introduced in line 281, "which says, 'I have encountered it . . . .'" This line is a singularly weighty chain of those morphemic words that look so much simpler than they are. But "which" seems to be no other than marriage itself, a voice from the whirlwind, offering testimony to itself, since Moore has used "which" here for the third time in a series beginning with a reference to "that striking grasp of opposites." The "it" of the line just preceding this one, "One sees that it is rare," is then equivalent to the "it" of "I have encountered it." The very trickiness of grammar at this point of the poem, as well as the last use of "says" in a definition, seems to demonstrate indeed that "Everything to do with love is mystery; / it is more than a day's work / to investigate this science." The great he/she debate about its features resolves into a self-testimony of the existence of union. But the mapping out of paradoxes and contradictions, while it may be called a "triumph of simplicity," hardly reveals "simplicity of temper"—at least, not in the poet.

In her finale, Moore invokes the figure of an orator again, but declares that "the debater and the Roman" are only superficial impostures. The true protégé of wisdom, while "seeming to parade" as these rhetoricians, is unpretentious, an archaic statesman, essentially simple in "temper," a term as slippery as "tone." Daniel Webster is the model for these types, but only in his role as park statue, with his perfect line beneath him as a caption: "Liberty and Union, now and forever." Whether Moore means to imply petrifaction of attitude or steadfastness of faith, or both, her semantic puzzles are only deepened, not destroyed, by irony. A feminist and suffragist in her youth, whose father left her mother with two infants, who herself never married, Moore arrives at no resolution within her definition. Even her least convoluted statements, those that seem to assure the reader of direction, may dance forward and back again without finality:

> Psychology which explains everything
> Explains nothing
> And we are still in doubt.

[ll. 18–20)

Both poet and reader are in doubt throughout the poem and after; to state the essence of a paradox only ensures continuation of the struggle to define, to find what words "perhaps one should say" of marriage.

Notes

1. Marianne Moore, *The Complete Poems of Marianne Moore* (New York: MacMillan/ Viking, 1967), pp. 62–70, 271–73. Bonnie Tymorski August, in "The Poetics of Woman-hood in Five Modern American Poets" (Ph. D. diss., New York University, 1978), points out that few of the quoted statements are about marriage. Moore chose them for effectiveness within her design rather than for relevance to her subject.

2. I use the version of "Marriage" from *Observations* (New York: Dial, 1924), a year after its initial publication (London: Maniken, 1923). The Maniken pamphlet version is rougher and less finished. Omitted from the second publication are quotations that seem a bit too long, lines that seem overdone (for example, in 1923, l. 184 read "one's self love's labor lost"; l. 198 read "to make a baby scholar, not a wife"). Versions after the second carry Moore's editing further without such good results; she has cut words and repetitions that provided meaningful resonance in their earlier positions. Such omissions, although not accidents, do constitute losses, for the purposes at least of this examination.

3. William Carlos Williams, "Marianne Moore," *Dial* 78 (May 1925): 399.

4. As in "Orchard": "you have flayed us / with your blossoms, / spare us the beauty / of fruit-trees," in *Selected Poems* (New York: Grove, 1957), p. 18.

5. Laurence Stapleton, *Marianne Moore: The Poet's Advance* (Princeton, N.J.: Princeton University Press, 1978), pp. 40–41.

6. Marianne Moore, "Idiosyncrasy and Technique," *A Marianne Moore Reader* (New York: Viking, 1961), p. 171: "If I may venture to say again what I have already said when obscurity was deplored, one should be as clear as one's natural reticence allows one to be." Compare "Humility, Concentration, Gusto," in the same collection, p. 123: "When I am as complete as I like to be, I seem unable to get an effect plain enough." And again, in an interview with Donald Hall, p. 261: "I think the most difficult thing for me is to be satisfactorily lucid, yet have enough implication in [a poem] to suit myself."